D1488984

The Creative Writing MFA Handbook

A GUIDE FOR PROSPECTIVE GRADUATE STUDENTS

Tom Kealey

continuum

NEW YORK • LONDON

Copyright © 2005 by Tom Kealey

The Continuum International Publishing Group
15 East 26th Street, New York, NY 10010

The Continuum International Publishing Group Ltd
The Tower Building, 11 York Road, London SE1 7NX

All rights reserved. No part of this book may be reproduced, stored in a retrieval system, or transmitted in any form or by any means, electronic, mechanical, including photocopying, recording, or otherwise, without the written permission of the publishers.

Cover design: Laurie Westhafer

Library of Congress Cataloging-in-Publication Data

Kealey, Tom.
The creative writing MFA handbook : a guide for prospective graduate students / Tom Kealey.
    p. cm.
  ISBN 0-8264-1843-0 (hardcover)—ISBN 0-8264-1817-1 (pbk.)
1. Creative writing (Higher education)—United States—Handbooks, manuals, etc. 2. Graduate students—United States—Handbooks, manuals, etc. I. Title.
  PE1405.U6K43 2005
  808'.042071173—dc22
                                        2005025228

Printed in the United States of America

05 06 07 08 09 10   10 9 8 7 6 5 4 3 2 1

*For my students
and
my teachers*

Contents

Preface

A GRADUATE PROGRAM IN CREATIVE WRITING offers either an M.A. (Master of Arts, one to two years), an M.F.A. (Master of Fine Arts, two to three-years) or a Ph.D. (Doctorate, five or more years) degree where students take writing workshops, craft and literature classes, and work on a book-length thesis of writing. Students explore their writing craft, interact within a community of peers and teachers, and most importantly take advantage of that greatest of gifts: time to write.

There are over 100 creative writing M.F.A. programs in the United States, over 100 M.A. programs with some sort of creative writing emphasis, and a handful, though a growing handful, of creative writing Ph.D. programs. These programs offer degrees primarily in fiction and poetry, though there are a number of universities that offer degrees in creative nonfiction, screenwriting, playwriting, children's literature, and even science writing.

This guide is, first and foremost, a friend of the prospective writing student, and it owes no allegiance to the graduate programs themselves. This guide is intended to be a trustworthy companion as you venture into the intriguing and sometimes intimidating world of what we call the Creative Writing M.F.A. (or M.A., or Ph.D.). I offer an overview of programs in general, and a more specific look at some programs in particular. More importantly, this guide will advise you during the critical stages of your graduate school search: researching, applying, and deciding. I'll answer as many questions as I can, and I'll try to be as definitive as possible.

I want you to think of me as the bus driver. You're on a bus tour in a new city: the city of graduate creative writing programs. I've lived here for a number of years, and I know my way around. I'm offering you an introduction to the city, and I hope a clear, useful, and entertaining introduction at that. I'll show you the highlights of this new city, I'll tell you which streets to avoid, I'll offer tips on how to best spend your time, and I'll even stop the bus a few times and take a closer look at particular neighborhoods. I've also brought along some other residents of the city, and they'll offer you some insights and recommendations as we move along. What I'm getting at is this: This guide is a starting point, and I intend it to be a good one. You'll understand the lay of the land once you're done with your tour. When you're done, I'm encouraging you to get out there into the city. I'm encouraging you to walk around, find the best neighborhoods and hotspots that meet your needs. And, I'll help you figure out what some of those needs are. It's my intention to get you started right, and equip you with the tools necessary to make the most of your experience.

So, this is what our tour will involve:

- The Basics. An overview of writing workshops. A breakdown of the differences between M.A., M.F.A., and Ph.D. programs. I'll talk about low-residency programs, and I'll define all sorts of terms like writing workshop, thesis defense, studio/academic, secondary language proficiency, and degree hour. I'll offer advice on where you should 'be' in your writing career when applying to graduate programs, and I'll explain the requirements of each degree.
- Criteria. To me, this is the most important chapter in the book. I want you to think about what you need from a creative writing program, because there are definite differences between each school. What sort of funding will you need? Would you like to be part of a small writing program or a large one? Will you concentrate exclusively on your writing, or do you want to take many literature and elective courses? I'll offer you a template of what a good writing program looks like, and I'll break down each of the criteria—location, funding, teaching, faculty, and others—so that you can decide what you need from your graduate experience.
- The Programs. I've profiled fifty creative writing programs. Though I strongly encourage you not to limit your search to these, this chapter will provide a good starting point for your search.

- The Application Process. Notes on the writing sample, letters of recommendation, the personal statement, the GREs, and the half-dozen other aspects of your application. I'll work to keep you organized and on task.
- Decision Time. Once you've applied to programs, you will undoubtedly be accepted and rejected in some combination. When all answers are in, it's time for you to make your decision. The criteria here are a little different from the original search criteria. I'll talk about how to make the best choice for you.
- Overview of the Program and Degree. I'll offer insight into the graduate experience so that you know what to expect, what to take advantage of, and what to avoid. I also include special sections on graduate teaching and publishing.
- A wonderful essay by writer Adam Johnson, "Counterpoint: A Guide to the M.F.A. and Beyond from an Outsider Who Became an Insider."
- Interviews with program directors, professors, and past and present graduate students.
- Links to graduate program reading lists online.
- Helpful Sources. Online and off.
- List of Programs. The most comprehensive list of graduate programs, in and outside the United States, with URL addresses and basic information.

So, before we get the bus rolling out of the lot, a brief introduction is in order. I graduated from the M.F.A. Creative Writing program at the University of Massachusetts in 2001, and afterwards I was a Wallace Stegner Fellow in fiction at Stanford University. I currently teach at Stanford. I've been in many, many writing workshops, both as a student and as a teacher. At the University of Massachusetts I was the recipient of the Distinguished Teaching Award. I'm thirty-five years old and, quite frankly, I wish there had been a book like this when I first thought about being a writer. I would have made more of my graduate experience, and I would have avoided some missteps. I have some strong opinions about what makes a good graduate writing program, and you'll definitely hear about them. My goal is to advise and inform. In the reverse order.

I expect that this book will cause some controversy in the creative writing community. Though that is not my goal, it is likely unavoidable. Others have strong opinions about their graduate experiences and their graduate schools. I respect those opinions, but I don't have any loyalty to them.

I'm in the prospective student's corner, and not in the corner of the programs themselves. I take my responsibilities as guide (and bus driver) very seriously. I hope this book will be helpful to you, and I hope you'll find some good neighborhoods and avoid some potholes.

In the end, the choice of a writing program, and what you make of the experience, will be yours. This guide offers the information and advice to help make those choices educated, organized, and enlightened.

Very special thanks to the professors, program directors, and current and former students I interviewed for this book, especially Aimee Bender, Michael Collier, Victoria Chang, Johanna Foster, Maria Hummel, Adam Johnson, Rachel Kadish, Scott McCabe, Heather McHugh, George Saunders, Tracy K. Smith, Bruce Snider, Peter Turchi, Padma Viswanathan, and Geoffrey Wolff. Their very helpful insights and advice appear throughout the book. The opinions expressed outside of their quotes (the rest of the book) are mine alone.

Finally, the acknowledgments section of the book thanks many people, but I'd like to say a special word here to David Roderick and Christina McCarroll, who offered insight and very helpful opinions throughout the many stages of this book. Thanks. You two are tops.

For more information and updates, check out the M.F.A. Weblog via TomKealey.com.

All right, people. Let's roll on out.

CHAPTER 1

The Basics

I WANT TO BEGIN by simply defining some terms and answering some specific questions.

Why apply to a creative writing program?

This is an important question, and one to which you may already know the answer. I'd like to offer my own answer, though, and I hope you'll keep it in mind throughout your application experience.

People often apply to programs for a variety of reasons: to complete a manuscript, to qualify themselves to teach on the college level, to live and work within a community of writers, and/or to escape back into academia from "the real world." But here's the real reason:

You're drawing a line in the sand, and you're saying, *I'm going to be a writer for the next few years, because I've always wanted to do that, and I'm going to see what I can make of myself.* Any reason above and beyond that may actually be a good reason, but that promise to yourself—that you're going to follow your muse and (at my risk of being melodramatic) your dream—is the key to making your experience work for you. If you don't have that, then there are a lot of other options in life, and perhaps you should consider them instead. By choosing the graduate program route, you are staking a claim to being a writer, and you're letting everyone around you know it. Lots of people talk about being a writer; you're doing something about it.

And of course on a more practical level you'll be developing your skills as a writer, you'll be studying your craft closely, and you'll be interacting with other students, writing teachers, and lots of good books in order to find your writing voice.

You are buying yourself time. And time is what a writer needs.

1

So, we need a degree in order to be writers?

Of course not. If you want to be a writer, write. If you want help along the way, then a graduate program might be a good fit for you.

Keep in mind that a creative writing degree, especially of the M.F.A. variety, is an artistic degree more than it is a professional degree. In this way it is similar to studio art degrees in sculpture, painting, and filmmaking.

Maria Hummel is a Stegner Fellow at Stanford University and graduate of the M.F.A. program at the University of North Carolina Greensboro

Q: Why apply to a creative writing program?
A: "One of the most important things I got out of the experience was time. Time to read and write, time to focus on the things I wanted to learn and develop. If you come straight from college, you may not appreciate that time as much, because you've always had it in school. It wasn't until I was out of college for two years that I understood what an incredible luxury it was to have two years of uninterrupted study. Everyone's background is different, but I recommend that people apply to programs when they have a body of interests or experiences that they want to explore through writing."

What are some aspects to a creative writing program?

These can vary of course. But your experience in a program will likely include the class work (writing workshops, literature courses, craft classes, electives), interaction with faculty (in class or sometimes in one-on-one tutorials), attending readings by visiting writers, the completion of a book-length manuscript, and very often your teaching of undergraduates in composition or creative writing classes. Programs may also have community outreach in the form of mentoring high school students or holding public readings by graduate students. Often, there are literary magazines connected with the program, where graduate students can gain editorial and publishing experience. And of course, there is the formal or informal literary community that generally emerges by placing so many writers in one place. The community atmosphere may take the form of readings by graduate students, informal workshops and reading groups, and parties and other social functions. I would expect you to make some friends in your program, many of them lifelong friends and fellow writers. And of course, you'll immerse yourself in reading and writing.

Where should I "be" in my writing career when applying to graduate programs?

Creative writing programs rarely expect your work to have been previously published. M.F.A. programs don't normally require you to have majored in English in your undergraduate work, though some Ph.D. and, to a lesser extent, M.A. programs, may expect this.

Basically, programs expect you to read a lot and write a lot. And this experience needs to be evident in the quality of your writing sample (part of your application, ten to thirty pages of your creative work). I'll emphasize this later, but do keep in mind that your writing sample is, by far, the most important element of your application. If the application readers (normally the professors of the program) like your work, then you have a great chance of being accepted. If they don't like your work, you have no chance.

I won't address the writing sample right now. I want to keep you, and me, on track. I'll address the writing sample and many other aspects in the application section.

Basically, you should be living a life that emphasizes literature and writing. What do I mean by that? Lots of things. If you took creative writing workshops and literature courses in your undergraduate work, then that helps. More importantly, those classes will give you a feel for what a graduate writing program will be like.

If you've never taken a writing workshop before, let me strongly encourage you to take a class soon. Writing classes are often taught as adult education classes at universities, at community colleges, online through extension courses (UCLA has a highly regarded online extension program), and at local neighborhood and community centers. Instructors of these classes are often M.F.A. graduates. I'm asking you to take these classes, now, for two reasons:

First, you'll get a clear idea of what your classroom experience will be like in graduate school. That's not to say that workshops aren't different from each other. Depending on the instructor and the other students, the atmosphere can be vastly different. However, the format is generally the same, and you'll know if this type of thing is what you want to be doing for the next two or three-years.

Second, if you have little experience in a writing community, you're not likely to get the type of letters of recommendation that can be most helpful for your graduate application. I'll talk more about letters later, but know that a recommendation from a writing teacher who knows your work well is the letter that selection committees will most listen to.

That said, there are many other ways to immerse yourself in your local writing community. Bookstores, libraries, and coffeehouses often hold readings, either of the open-mike variety or scheduled readers. Pick up a schedule and go to these events. If you live near a university, there are likely to be events there as well. Make a phone call to the English department. Writers groups are another good way to be thinking and doing something about your writing. Writers groups have similarities to workshops, but are less formal, and that can often be a good thing. Check your local newspaper or bulletin boards at coffeehouses and cafes.

And of course, read. Read a lot and write a lot. That's the best way to hone your craft. For links to reading lists, including the excellent one developed by the Gotham Writers' Workshop, do consult Appendix B of this book.

My point in all of this? *Be around* writing, and your writing will improve. And when your writing is improved, you have a better chance of being accepted to graduate programs.

What is the average age of a creative writing graduate student?

That's a good question. There's no data that I'm aware of, but in my nonscientific poll of a dozen former graduate students, the age that came up the most often was twenty-eight. Everyone said there were younger students—straight out of college—and much more experienced students in their thirties and forties. But twenty-eight sounds about right to me, as far as an average goes. There are definitely fifty-plus-year-olds who are pursuing their craft after many years as professionals and/or parents.

But that brings up a point I'd like to make: I don't think it's wise to apply to graduate programs straight out of undergraduate studies. Why not? It's been my observation that these students tend to burn out without having a break from their academic studies. Other people will tell you: "You've got to have life experience before you write." While I agree with that, I also know that there are many twenty-year-olds who have much greater life experiences than some fifty-year-olds. That said, taking a break from academia to work, travel, volunteer, teach, or whatever you want, is highly recommended. At the very least, time away from school will help you appreciate the benefits of the academic world. A two-year break between undergraduate and graduate seems sufficient and wise to me.

What is a writing workshop?

The writing workshop is the backbone of any creative writing program. Students generally take four workshops in their concentration (fiction, poetry, nonfiction etc.). A typical workshop holds ten to sixteen graduate students and one professor. Most workshops will meet once a week, but in some programs workshops meet twice a week. Students turn in poems and stories, the rest of the class reads them, and during the following class, "workshop" happens. Basically, the writer remains silent while the class discusses the work in detail. In other words, the writer gets to sit in while the class holds an editorial-type meeting about the work. (Generally, the class will sit around one large table). Questions that might arise are: What are the strengths of this work? What ground is it covering? What were we confused about in the work? What suggestions do we have for improving it? What was our reaction to the work in general and to the voice in particular?

At the end of the workshop, the writer is often allowed to ask questions of the class, either to clarify what has been already said or to cover territory that was not yet discussed. A workshop for a fifteen-page story might last around thirty to forty minutes. The workshop for a one-page poem will last around ten minutes. Obviously, poetry workshops cover more submissions per class.

I'll discuss workshop in greater detail in a later chapter of this book, but for now consider that workshops are an opportunity to hear the reactions and opinions of your readers. It's an opportunity to have some of your assumptions reinforced and other assumptions challenged. You'll get another "take" on your writing, and through that process you can work to improve it. Perhaps most importantly, workshop provides a way to identify key readers—people who understand what you are trying to do and who can help you achieve it—that you can lean on during your graduate experience and throughout your writing life.

What do you mean when you say "literature" course?

I mean classes where you'll study books, write papers about them, and discuss them in class. There are also "craft" classes, which are a type of literature class, but focused more closely on the writer's perspective. For example, a literature class studying Virginia Woolf's *Mrs. Dalloway* may focus on the time period, social norms, historical events, gender and class issues, and linguistic influences that impacted the book. Meanwhile, a craft class studying the same book might focus on the choices and techniques Woolf uses to construct the language and narrative. Many literature classes are blends of craft classes, and in many craft classes students will work on imitations (writing in the voice of the author) or other writing assignments (with a focus, say, on voice, form, narration, dialogue, or description).

Obviously, workshop, craft, and literature classes can vary, depending on the instructor and the program, and the students, for that matter. But the important distinction to remember is that a *workshop* class will focus on in-progress student writing, while a *literature* or *craft* class will focus on published writing.

What are the requirements of a graduate degree?

These will vary from program to program, but generally the requirements will include writing workshops, craft classes, literature classes, electives, and a book-length thesis. Some programs require proficiency in a secondary language, others require a defense of the thesis before a committee, and others require a reading list and graduate exam. I'll address the three types of degrees here in *very* general terms:

M.A. degree—Master of Arts. One to two years. Six to twelve classes. About a 3:1 ratio between literature classes and writing workshops. A master's exam on a specific reading list is almost always required, as is a final creative thesis. A secondary language proficiency is often required. Most M.A. degrees concentrate on the study of literature first and the crafting of writing second, so it's an appropriate degree for students who want to immerse themselves in literature but who still want to write creatively.

M.F.A. degree—Master of Fine Arts. Two to three-years. Eight to sixteen classes. Four writing workshops are almost always required, as are about an equal number of literature courses. Many programs offer classes in the craft of writing, and other programs encourage students to take electives in other departments such as art, psychology, history, and others. A creative thesis (book length) is always required. A secondary language and a master's exam in literature may be required, but not often. This is an appropriate degree for students who wish to focus primarily on their own writing, with secondary emphasis on literature and other classes.

Ph.D. degree—Doctor of Philosophy. Five or more years. Ten to eighteen classes. Two advanced exams (one written, one oral) related to reading lists are normally required, as is a secondary language proficiency and a final creative dissertation and its defense. Generally speaking, this is a Ph.D. degree in English with a secondary emphasis in creative writing. Many Ph.D. programs will accept credits that students earned during their M.A. or M.F.A. study. This is an appropriate degree for students who want to study literature at an advanced, intensive level, and who wish to work on their own writing for some of that time.

Do these vary from program to program?

Yes, very much so. Some M.F.A. degrees in creative writing may actually lean more toward the literature side, as opposed to the creative writing side. Meanwhile, there are some Ph.D. and M.A. programs that concentrate primarily on writing. The bottom line: A program's list of requirements and classes will give you a clear sense of the emphasis of the degree.

I'll give you a rule of thumb: Something close to a 2:1 or 1:1 ratio of literature and writing workshops is a program concentrating in creative writing. Something closer to a 3:1 ratio or higher is a program concentrating in literature.

Keep in mind that programs which offer a fair number of electives (two or more) offer students the best flexibility, because students can choose their own concentration: literature, writing classes, or classes outside the English department.

Are there other terms for these concentrations?

Yes. They are "Studio" for concentrations in writing and craft classes, and "Academic" for writing degrees concentrating in literature. And of course, there is the hybrid "Studio/Academic." These terms are not often used, but from time to time you'll see them on a program's Web site. Now you know what they mean.

What is a degree hour?

That's easy. Sort of.

One class generally equals three degree hours. In other words, a 24 hour master's degree will equal eight classes. However, it does get tricky: often "thesis hours" are given for work on the longer writing project, and sometimes workshops and non-workshop classes will count as six degree hours. Bottom line: Be clear about how many total *classes* a program requires, rather than how many degree hours.

Can you, like, give us an example of a program's requirements, so we know what you're talking about?

Sure. Let's take a quick trip to the University of Michigan's Web site. It's available at http://www.lsa.umich.edu/english/grad/mfa/.

The University of Michigan is a two-year M.F.A. program in fiction or poetry. The program is 36 degree hours, and in this case that means four workshops, four literature classes, plus thesis hours (work toward your book-length manuscript). The Web site indicates that there is some flexibility in changing one literature class to a class outside the department. A secondary language proficiency is required, as is a final thesis.

My conclusion, therefore (based on the 1:1 ratio), is that the program concentrates on the writing aspect, as opposed to primarily on the literature aspect. As an aside, I like the flexibility that the program offers in choosing your classes.

What is a thesis defense?

Oh, man, we are getting off track here. Quickly: Not all programs will required a thesis defense, but I think it's an important aspect to a program. You write a collection of stories or poems (or a novel or screenplay or play, etc.). A fiction/nonfiction thesis will be 120 pages or more. A poetry thesis will be 40 pages or more. You choose a committee of three professors to read it, then you "defend" it in a thesis meeting. Basically, you'll be asked questions about your literary vision, voice, decisions, and goals. Some people are intimidated by this process, but I don't think that is necessary. Check it out: One of those committee members will be your advisor. And your advisor will tell you when your manuscript is ready to be defended. I've often heard of students who have had to rework their manuscript on the advice of the advisor (before the defense; this might take an extra semester). But I've rarely heard of a student who fails his/her thesis defense. Generally speaking, the purpose of the committee and defense is to challenge and encourage (in some combination or another) your overall creative graduate work.

Many programs will use only a thesis advisor and not a committee, and that may work out just fine.

However, if a program does not require a thesis at all, then that's a program not particularly interested in your work.

Do most programs require a secondary language proficiency?

Almost all Ph.D. programs will require a secondary language proficiency, and so will many M.A. programs. As for the M.F.A. programs, I'd say that about 20 percent require a secondary language proficiency. Proficiency might be measured in the form of an exam, coursework, or translation. And if a program does not require a language proficiency, but you still wish to learn a second or third language, my guess is that you can use your electives to take language and translation classes. Bottom line: There is flexibility for people interested in secondary languages, and for people who are terrified of them. Just be sure to check a program's requirements and class flexibility.

When you say Ph.D., M.F.A., and M.A. programs in this book, do you always mean creative writing programs (or programs that have an emphasis in creative writing), or do you sometimes mean programs in English or other subjects?

I always mean creative writing programs. If I mean another subject, including English with no creative writing aspect, then I'll indicate it.

What is a low-residency program?

Outstanding question. Low-residency programs are a small but quickly expanding type of program. They are almost exclusively M.F.A. programs.

Low-residency programs are a type of distance-learning degree in creative writing. You don't have to be present at the university full time in order to obtain a degree.

I really like the idea behind low-residency programs, as they allow a great flexibility for students who have family or career responsibilities where they currently live. Here's how they work: Generally speaking, a student is matched with a teacher for a semester. The student receives a reading list from the teacher, and the student also sends stories or poems and revisions of these stories and poems to the teacher throughout the semester. The teacher sends back comments and suggestions. It's basically a long-distance one-on-one workshop. Communication may be through e-mail, post, or phone, depending on the teacher's preference. Classes are not necessarily limited to the "workshop" type, and literature classes may be offered. Either way, there is an expanding reading list that the student must complete and report on.

In most cases, each semester will begin with a seven- to ten-day conference, where *all* of the students and *all* of the teachers actually do attend the university and hold workshops, seminars, and classes. Sometimes these conferences take place over the summer. In any case, these events are intensive, required for the degree, and, from what I've heard, a lot of fun.

The upside to low-residency programs are that they offer great time flexibility (a degree can be completed over the course of a few or many years), and they offer great one-on-one relationships with other writers. The two biggest downsides are: 1. There is less of a "visible" community of writers, though there is a community in its own way, especially during the conferences, and 2. Very rarely is funding available for students. Students pay their way through the course of the program. A four-semester low-residency course of study will cost $20,000 or more.

Either way, the low-residency programs are an excellent option for students who wish to concentrate on their writing without moving to a new location.

Rachel Kadish teaches in the Lesley University M.F.A. program. Her work includes *From a Sealed Room* and *Soon Also for You*.

Q: From a teacher's perspective, how does the low-residency format work?

A: "I don't know whether writing can be taught, but I believe it can be coached, like athletics can be coached. I'll stand on my head for my students, but they've got to run the laps themselves. What I love about the low-residency setup is that I meet with each student. They tell me what they need as a writer, and I'll tell them what I observe. We agree on what they will read. They do craft annotations. I focus on different things for different students. They read this novel or these short stories. It's very individualized, and you can see a real blossoming during the course of a semester. I encourage students to pay close attention to what interests them. You can see a big change in just a few months."

Scott McCabe is a recent graduate of the Lesley University M.F.A. program:

Q: What advice would you offer students who are considering the low-residency format?
A: "What's important is really considering the nature of the programs themselves. You have to be realistic about how much self-teaching goes into it. There are an entirely different set of benefits and problems that go along with this kind of program. You get to know your teachers extremely well. The mentoring aspect is very strong. On the other hand, you're disconnected from your peers for much of the year. It takes more to stay motivated. At the same time, it's good preparation for the actual life of a writer. Students should understand both sides of the experience."

Are there graduate programs in creative writing outside the United States?

Definitely. Over forty of them by my count, and there are likely more. The majority are found in Canada and the United Kingdom, though Australia, New Zealand, the Philippines, Mexico, Spain, and the Republic of Korea are also represented. You can find information about these particular programs in Appendix D of this book.

Though the information found in this handbook is aimed primarily at students interested in programs within the United States, the majority of the information is applicable to programs in other countries. The basic ideas of workshop, funding, teaching, the application, criteria, and others will be applicable no matter where a student applies.

Most graduate schools accept students from other countries, so no matter where you call home, do consider programs in areas of the world where you'd like to live. Do keep in mind a university and country's requirements for limited residency. A university Web site should hold this information. Do contact program coordinators directly, and do allow for more time in the application process.

What can you tell us about funding?

I can tell you a lot, and most of what I'll tell you will be in the next chapter. That said, a sneak preview is this: In my opinion (and in the opinion of most writers and graduate students), funding from the program is critical to your graduate experience. Many programs offer funding to students in the form of writing fellowships and teaching assistantships. In these cases, your tuition is waived and you receive a stipend of anywhere from $5,000 to $15,000.

I'd say that about 20 percent of programs fund *all or most* of their students. Another 40 percent fund *some* of their students, and the remaining 40 percent fund *only a few or none* of their students. The discrepancy in funding has more to do with resources than anything else. Most graduate students in other fields pay for their graduate study. That said, a program with resources—financial and otherwise—is a program you want

Keep in mind that a year's tuition at a private school may be upwards of $30,000, while tuition at a public in-state school may be only $5,000. And there is everything in between. Needless to say, a tuition waiver sometimes goes a long way.

You know better than I do about your funding needs. If you are independently wealthy, then you've got a lot of options. Otherwise, a basic principle of this book is to encourage students to seek programs that offer funding. If funding is not available, I'm encouraging students to aim their sites at *affordable* programs, rather than expensive ones. More about that next chapter. And in every chapter for that matter.

What will be included in my application packet, and are we back on track now?

Yes, we've been back on track for the last few questions. Thanks for asking.

Sorry to keep saying "More on this later, but here's a quick preview," but I want this chapter to be an overview and subsequent chapters to dive into specifics.

Application requirements may vary. But generally speaking, an M.F.A. program will require a writing sample (about 25 pages of prose or 15 of poetry), three letters of recommendation, a personal statement, undergraduate transcripts, GRE scores, and the application form itself. Some M.F.A. programs will require a critical essay in some form.

For Ph.D. programs and some M.A. programs add to that list the GRE Literature subject scores and definitely the critical essay.

My bet is that no two of your potential programs will ask for the same materials in the same order, so keeping track of all of these elements is essential.

Bruce Snider holds the M.F.A. in poetry and playwriting from The University of Texas Michener Center, where he later served as graduate coordinator for admissions and advising. His first book of poetry is *The Year We Studied Women*.

Q: How many programs should students apply to?
A: "Well, I think a lot. As many as you can afford to apply to. I applied to ten or twelve. That was a pretty good number. So much of the admissions process is subjective. You want to increase the chances of your work finding a sympathetic reader. The more applications you put out there, the more likely you are to get into a program with funding, in a place you'd like to live."

How many programs will we be applying to?

Why beat around the bush here? You'll apply to eight to twelve programs. Why? Because I said so. And because, for the most part, you can't predict who will like your writing sample and who will not. And if you apply to three programs and none of those readers likes your writing sample, then you have no options. Instead, spread your net wide. Keep your options open. I can tell you this: I applied to five schools, and when I got rejected by the first three and waitlisted for the fourth, I definitely wish I'd applied to more. Don't be a dummy like me.

Keep in mind that the application fee for each school will be $40–65 dollars. Sure, that adds up, but hey, this is your life here. Make the investment in yourself.

When are the deadlines for applications?

They begin in the beginning of December and go as late as mid-February. Make sure you know the deadlines for your particular schools and stick to them. The vast majority of deadlines will fall in January.

How do I choose my best writing sample?

Sorry. No preview on that. See chapter 4.

What criteria should I use for selecting programs where I'll apply?

All right, a very short preview on this. The next chapter is focused almost exclusively on this question.

In order: 1. location (where will you live, work, and grow during these years?); 2. funding (will you receive funding or will you pay for your graduate education?); 3. teaching opportunities (is this important to you, and if so, what sort of opportunities for teaching are available to you?); 4. faculty (who will you be working with during your years in the program?); 5. other aspects, including program size and degree flexibility.

That's a lot of information in one chapter. Can we get a summary?

No problem.

Chapter Summary

1. There are many reasons to apply to a creative writing program, but the main reason is to provide yourself the time and space to actually *be* a writer, instead of simply hoping to be one. Other reasons include teaching experience, the writing community, and, of course, developing your skills as a writer.

2. The three types of degrees are the M.A., the M.F.A., and the Ph.D. There are more than one hundred M.A. programs in the United States and also more than one hundred M.F.A. programs. There are about two dozen Ph.D. programs with emphases in creative writing. An M.A. program is generally one to two years. An M.F.A. is generally two to three-years, and a Ph.D. is five years or more. All programs will include some form of coursework (writing workshops, literature classes, craft classes, and electives), interaction with faculty, readings by visiting writers, the completion of a book-length manuscript, and very likely some form of teaching. Other aspects may include community outreach, a final graduate exam and reading list, a secondary language proficiency, working on the editorial board of a literary magazine, and public readings.

3. Low-residency programs are a good fit if you have a full-time job you intend to keep, or if you cannot travel to another location for

family or career reasons. Most low-residency programs require two annual ten-day residencies on campus with faculty and other students, and then the rest of the year students are matched one-on-one with writing teachers who direct their study through e-mail or mail correspondence.

4. Workshops are the backbone of creative writing programs. Workshops offer writers a chance to hear reactions and suggestions about their work from a class of their peers and teachers. Literature classes, craft classes, and electives make up the remainder of the coursework.

5. An application to a creative writing program will include some combination of a writing sample, three letters of recommendation, a personal statement, undergraduate transcripts, GRE scores, and, in some cases, a critical essay and GRE subject scores.

6. Potential students should apply to eight to twelve schools, and funding should be a top priority when researching programs.

CHAPTER 2

What to Look for in a Creative Writing Program

THE BEST CREATIVE WRITING PROGRAMS have good support—financial and otherwise—for their graduate students, and they provide a variety of opportunities in the classroom, in teaching experience, and in publishing. I've listed below what I consider to be the most important elements of a solid creative writing program. I'd doubt that any one program will get high marks on *all* of these aspects, but do keep these things in mind. A solid program will provide most of these opportunities. Some aspects may be more important to you than others, and some of them might not be relevant if, for example, you're seeking a low-residency M.F.A. In any case, I'd encourage you to create your own list of "must-haves" when you're making your initial and final selections.

Financial support. A solid resident program provides full funding for most, if not all, its graduate students in the form of fellowships, teaching assistantships, editing and research assistantships, and scholarships. Programs that fund all of their students are in the minority, but at the very least programs should have affordable tuition and should seek additional funding sources for their students.

Teaching experience. The program should provide an opportunity for graduate students to teach at least one year of college or creative writing.

Faculty. An acceptable teacher/student ratio is 1 to 12. Lower is better, of course. Faculty should have consistent publications and a consistent record of teaching excellence. You can easily find a list of faculty publications by searching the Web. A measure of teaching excellence is best discovered by speaking with current students in the program, and I'd encourage you to hold off on that until you are actually accepted to the program. Students are much more likely to spend time with you then, and the idea of "teaching excellence" is more important to your final decision than it is to your preliminary list of programs.

Class size. The best workshop size is 10–12 graduate students.

Literary magazines and presses. The existence of a literary magazine connected with the school or program (and/or a small university press) will likely provide editorial experience and internships. A healthy writing program is connected to the writing field outside the university.

Visiting writers. A program that brings three to four or more visiting writers a year is the sign of a healthy financial program. Big names are good, though some rising stars are more likely to visit classrooms and give students some face time.

Community outreach. At the University of Massachusetts we had a program through the Writers in Schools organization where M.F.A. students visited classrooms in local high schools. This was terrific experience, and a lot of fun, and it showed that the program had a good reputation in the community. Other community outreach could include programs for the elderly, prisons, writer groups, and youth societies.

Graduate student readings. To me, this is a real key for judging how serious the program takes its graduate students. When I lived in North Carolina, I'd often attend the UNCG M.F.A. program thesis readings. One poet and one fiction writer (both M.F.A. students) would hold a reading, sponsored by the university, in their final year of the program. It was a big deal. Lots of undergraduates, faculty, and often the M.F.A. students' parents (flying in from the other side of the country) would attend. It was very clear that the graduate students were highly valued by the program. Meanwhile, at UMass Amherst, we were left to create a reading series on our own at a local bookstore. Which was actually a lot of fun, but hey, a program could do *both*. In any case, a strong graduate student reading series—on or off campus—gets high marks from me. It shows that a program is committed to and celebrates and values its students and their creative work.

Contacts with editors and agents. This sounds like a big thing and, yes, it can be a big thing. But it's not likely to be promoted on the Web site. This is another question to ask current students. Formal or informal seminars about magazine publishing and the business of writing (offered by faculty or visitors) is another sign of a solid program.

Student publications. If current or previous graduate students are publishing books and in magazines, then the Web site should be highlighting this information. This is another big key for me. While publication does not necessarily equate with excellence, a program should be interested in promoting its students' creative work.

Courses within the department. A list of graduate classes should be available from the Web site (If not, then do contact the program coordinator.) A solid list of literature classes is always a good thing. Literature classes aimed specifically at writers is even better. Classes about publishing and editing is a terrific sign for a program.

Courses outside the department. Some flexibility in attending classes outside the department, I think, is an important element of a graduate student experience. Two "flexible" classes (six degree hours normally) is about right.

Graduating students. The program should graduate a high number of its incoming students. Keep in mind that creative writers are a fickle group. Some arrive at a program and decide that the *life*, not necessarily the program, is not right for them. An 85 percent graduation rate is acceptable. Anything lower is not necessarily a deal-breaker, but it's a question you should explore with current students. The program coordinator should have these statistics. If he/she doesn't, then ask to be referred to the right person at the graduate school. Again, this is something you should consider during your final choice.

The library. A well-stocked university library is always a good thing. A program library, like the excellent one at the University of Virginia, is an even better sign that the program takes its students' research and reading seriously. Oftentimes programs will have their holdings in the main library.

Graduate student representation on committees. I'm not talking about thesis committees, which I'll discuss next. I'm talking about committees that help plan and coordinate the program's yearly events, visitors, and functions. I'm also talking about graduate student representation on committees that set long-term goals for the program. To me, this is a real key for determining how seriously a program takes its students. I certainly don't expect a graduate student to be put in charge of the budget. (Ha.) But a program that doesn't get input from its graduate students is a program completely out of touch with its biggest population. Noy Holland at UMass often placed students on program committees, and they offered good insight into the needs and contributions of the graduate population. A solid program has two or three student representatives on a variety of planning committees. This type of information is not likely available on the Web site, though it *should* be. Ask the program coordinator about student representation.

Thesis. A final thesis is often required for graduation. The thesis consists of the student's chosen creative work from his or her time at the institution. Basically, it's a book, or part of a book, of creative work. A solid program always requires a thesis. Some programs will call this something else (a project, a manuscript, etc.), and that's fine. Bottom line: One advisor and perhaps a small committee of faculty should be reading and giving feedback (criticism and encouragement) about the student's completed work. A program that does not require a final thesis is a program that is not very interested in the career of the student.

Final note: I want to reiterate here: It's likely that no program has *all* of these elements. But the best programs will have most of them. Keep them in mind as a checklist, and as a measurement for your future program.

CRITERIA

By the end of this chapter, you should understand what criteria you will use to select your programs, and you should also know where to go to find the information you need about the individual schools.

For the most part, you'll find information about the particular programs on their university's Web site. I've listed all the creative writing programs at the back of this book along with some basic information, including their Web addresses. Keep in mind that information can change from year to year, and so it's in your best interests to consult the program Web sites.

One note on the Web sites: In my opinion, a poorly designed Web site indicates a poorly designed creative writing program. This is the twenty-first century. Program directors should be seeking the best applicants by making their information clear and accessible. A good Web site need not be flashy or filled with bells and whistles. But the information prospective students are seeking—about faculty, funding, curriculum, etc.—should be clear and straightforward. A phone number and contact e-mail should also be readily available. For more information about what a program Web site should contain, please see "Note to Program Directors" in chapter 3.

What sort of criteria should we use in selecting and applying to programs?

I'm going to swim directly against the tide of conventional wisdom about how to select the program that is right for you. Most articles and advice about programs have centered on faculty, encouraging prospective students to seek out the best faculty writers and to choose their program in accordance with this. But what is not often mentioned, but what should be obvious, is that the "best" writers don't often make the best teachers. Certainly sometimes they do, but often the biggest name writers in a program teach only one class a year. Keep in mind that professors can be on sabbatical and, even more often, they move from program to program, so the faculty you begin with may not be the faculty you end with. It simply doesn't make sense to me to make a two- to three-year life choice based primarily on the faculty criteria. So, while most advice is to place faculty first in your decision, I am strongly encouraging you to place it about fourth.

So what's the first criteria, then?

Hold on. I first want to state the obvious, in case it is not so for some prospective students. In many ways, you'll first focus your search based on your genre. If you're interested in fiction or poetry, then you have hundreds of options. If creative nonfiction is your interest, there are dozens of programs that can accommodate you.

The genres of screenwriting, playwriting, children's literature and others are much more limited. So, keep this in mind. I'm not counting it as a criteria to explore, because I'm assuming you already know your genre. I've listed the genres offered by each school in Appendix D.

Okay. So what's the first criteria?

Location. Where do you want to live? Where will you be most comfortable and challenged as a writer? You'll spend the majority of your time in the program *alone*, writing. Make sure your environment is one that you like, and one that you can build a life within. Do you want to live in a big city or a small town? Do you want to live on one of the coasts and, if so, which one? Do you need lots of sunshine, or snow, or nightlife, or nature? Considering these questions first and foremost will help narrow your search from a hundred programs to a more manageable number.

And, I offer some cautionary advice: Definitely make a list of the places you want to live, but also make a list of, as writer Steve Almond says, "the places where you *could stand* to live." Though I think location is the most important initial criteria, it's not the only one. Keep your needs in mind, but also keep your options open.

We thought you said funding was important. Where does that fit on the list?

It's right here, at number two. Keep in mind: You're narrowing your list of potential programs, not making your final selection. Funding might be number one on your list as you make your final decision on where to attend.

That said, how much do you want to pay for your creative writing degree? If you are independently wealthy, then perhaps Columbia—a university with an outstanding reputation—is the right one for you. At $33,000 a year, with little chance for a fellowship or tuition waiver, you'll be $66,000 in the hole after two years, and since some students stay for three, you might be as much as $100,000 in the hole. Plus the expenses of living in New York City.

Well, you can see what my attitude is towards these types of programs. I don't like schools that charge exorbitant amounts to study writing. Why not? First of all, there are many other schools that do offer funding, or that offer affordable tuition. Second, if you're going to be a writer, you should get in the habit of living cheaply, at least till you sell a few books, which may be a number of years away. And third, and very important in my mind, is that expensive programs tend to have less diverse workshops. I'm not talking particularly about racial diversity or gender diversity; I'm talking about life diversity. People from many different parts of the country and the world who have had different experiences to share within the workshop. In many ways, I am talking about economic diversity.

As Johanna Foster, a potential M.F.A. student, points out, a program that charges very high tuition is likely to get three kinds of students: "The rich, the very rich, and the financially irresponsible." And that's not to say that these three groups might not have much to offer a workshop; it's just that there's no sense in limiting your peers to these three groups.

Why do programs charge tuition?

Most graduate students outside of creative writing pay in full for their education. Running a university and running a program requires money. Much of this money comes from tuition, though many programs are funded through a combination of donors and grants. Many schools fund their students through teaching assistantships, where graduate students teach composition and creative writing to undergraduates.

My point: There are funding options out there. You may end up paying tuition for your creative writing education, and that's fine. But make sure it's affordable to your budget, and before you pay, explore your options.

What about programs that fund some students and don't fund others?

These programs are limited financially, as are most graduate programs in a variety of fields. Education costs money. The tuition of some students pays for the existence of the program.

That said, I want to caution you about what I'll call "tiered" funding. Tiered funding offers fellowships for writing, teaching, or research to *some* students, and requires tuition from other students. Again, this is a necessity for many programs. However, I'm concerned about the competitive atmosphere that arises in some of these programs.

For example, let's take the State College of Nowhere. This university accepts thirty students each year. Ten students are fully funded through writing and teaching fellowships; ten students are partially funded through the same means (half a tuition waiver, or a stipend that covers three quarters, a half, or a quarter of tuition); and ten students pay full tuition and fees.

So, who determines who gets the ten full fellowships? The program director chooses, with perhaps some input from the other professors.

This is fine if you're in the top funding third, but there's a catch: There is sometimes a "re-ranking" of students in the second year. So while you may start out in the top third, you may end up partially funded in the second year, or even paying full tuition. How are these re-rankings determined? That's hard to say, and even program directors (who, again, are often forced to make these decisions because of budgetary constraints) might not be able to say. What we hear most is: "Potential as a writer." And what is that based on? Lots of things: The quality of your writing in workshop, your ability to get your work published in magazines, your ability as a student, and very likely your ability to network with and influence the people in a position to make these choices.

My point? Programs that are forced to "tier" the funding of their students often create very competitive atmospheres and relationships between their graduate students. For example, if you're in the running for one of the top spots, what kind of workshop critiques will you offer students who you are competing with? What will you say about their work in the presence of faculty members (who will be ranking the students at the end of the year)? What will other students say about your work? Will you be likely to offer your time and friendship to people with whom you are in direct competition? Will they offer you this time and friendship?

In a perfect world, perhaps. Keep in mind that as a writer you are in competition with yourself. You are always trying to improve your craft and voice. You shouldn't spend time worrying whether you're a "better" writer than your colleagues. "Better" is subjective, and writers are different rather than "better" or "worse." However, I want you to keep this competitive funding atmosphere in mind. I don't see that it is helpful for most writers, though it may be unavoidable for many programs.

Am I clear? If not, when you're narrowing your initial choices, do some "tiering" of your own. Fully funded programs first, partially funded programs second, and low-funded programs last.

Are there other forms of financial aid?

Yes. There are loans, of course, some university-wide grants, and of course there is in-state tuition. If you end up attending a public university, you should plan on taking the steps to become a resident as soon as you are accepted. You should also fill out the FASA (the Free Application for Federal Student Aid), which will greatly help your eligibility for a variety of funding sources. For the most part, the majority of the available funding will come directly through the creative writing program or the English department.

Do look at Appendix C for information on FASA and also the Jacob Javits Fellowship.

Do tuition and fees vary greatly between programs?

Oh yes. Obviously, tuition will be higher at private colleges and sometimes significantly lower at public institutions. Less tuition if you are a resident of a particular state. Do keep in mind that you can gain residency in a short or long period of time, depending on the state.

I think it's a very good idea to lean towards public universities if finances will be an issue for you.

We're confused now, and discouraged.

I'm sorry. I didn't mean to discourage or confuse anyone, least of all you. Let me be clear: Around 20 percent of programs fund all or most of their graduate students. Around 40 percent fund most or some of their graduate students. And around 40 percent of programs fund some or none of their students. Obviously, some creative writing graduate students in the country will be funded, and others will not. The tuition at public universities are more affordable than those at private universities. I'm asking you to keep your financial needs in mind, and to rank your schools accordingly.

In the next chapter I'll profile around fifty programs, and I'll be as clear as I can about funding. In the meantime, you can get a very good feel for the funding level of a program by visiting its Web site. Look under tuition, financial aid, or fellowships. If a school offers funding to the majority of its students, then the Web site will state this. If the program does not offer funding at all, or if it has a clearcut "tiered" system, then it will likely be vague about funding. I'm encouraging you to lean towards the programs that state their funding information clearly.

Do you feel better now?

A little. Thanks.

No problem.

So, location is first, and funding is second. What's third?

Third is teaching. I'm a big fan of acquiring teaching experience during your graduate program years. It's essential if you plan on teaching after the program, and even if you're not planning on teaching later, you still learn a lot from your students. I think Thomas E. Kennedy puts it best: "There is no doubt that teaching is the best way to learn because it forces you to test your assumptions and see if they're really true."

It's my opinion that you don't really understand a subject completely until you have to teach it to others.

In my first creative writing class I remember telling students that it's more important for your characters to be vulnerable, rather than "tough." Why? Because in real life we certainly like our friends and family members because of their strengths, but we also love them for their weaknesses as well. It's both, and you can ask any parent that. Meanwhile, on the page, we like characters who make mistakes, who use bad judgment, who say the wrong things, and we also like it when they work their way out of these situations. Or work their way deeper into a hole. In any case, I remember saying this, and I can remember a student, Sylvie, who asked, "Well, *how* do you make your characters vulnerable?"

A good question, and one I did not have the answer to. It's one thing to make a statement and it's another thing to prove it and show it, which is what teaching is much about. The next class, I brought in an excerpt from "The Point" by Charles D'Ambrosio. It's about a boy, thirteen years old, who guides drunk adults along a beach at night so that they don't fall in the water and drown. It's actually about much more than that, but for the purpose of this little aside, let's leave it at that. The boy, Kurt, is smart, he's capable, he's focused, he thinks these adults are ridiculous, but he's very serious about his job and he does it better than anyone in the world. A tough kid. While his adult companions are sobbing drunk about their failed marriages, their poor financial investments, their distant relationships with their children, Kurt's response is always, "There's time to think about that tomorrow. For now, let's just get you home."

But there's this wonderful moment near the middle of the story when Kurt relates to the reader his theory of "The Black Hole." The black hole is, like the imploded star in space, a great vacuum in your life, and it's constantly pulling on you, drawing you in, trying to suck the life out of you. His father, he feels, fell into this black hole the year before. "He shot himself in the head one morning—did I already say this?" he relates to us. And later, "You understand, I miss Father, miss having him around to tell me what's right and what's wrong, or to talk about boom-boom, which is sex, or just to go salmon fishing out by Hat Island and not worry about things." Suddenly, at these moments, the story opens up and breathes for us. We see some things very clearly, not the least of which is that Kurt feels an enormous guilt for allowing his father to fall into his depression, into his black hole, and Kurt's job, guiding these often ridiculous drunks home, is a way to make amends for this. It's touching, at least to me, because there's no reason a thirteen-year-old should have to feel guilty about being a poor "guide" to adults, and yet Kurt feels this clearly and deeply.

In any case, we talked about this in class, I pointed out some things I could see, and students pointed out some things I never would have. I knew it was important to make your characters vulnerable, but I only had the slightest knowledge of how to actually *do* it on the page. I'm not saying I'm an expert now, but I'm closer thanks to that particular student's question, and thanks to my own work in thinking and planning before class.

So, I think teaching is very helpful to a writer, and I'd encourage you to seek out these opportunities in your graduate program. I taught composition long before I taught creative writing, and I learned much from my students and myself during this time as well.

My point? If you want to improve your writing, and increase your chances of funding, and gain experience in teaching, then keep your eye on programs that offer opportunities for teaching assistantships.

And by the way, assistantships vary. You may be in charge of a class. You may be assisting a professor with a larger class. Both have their advantages.

But if we teach, we'll have less time for our writing.

True. And not true. Teaching takes time away from your writing. Teaching can take up a lot of time. One class, especially during your first semester (when you're figuring things out), can take up to 20–25 hours a week in grading, preparing, commenting, and all the other things that go along with running a classroom.

On the other hand, for some people, if you are forced to be organized in the classroom, you'll learn skills about being organized in your writing time. When I'm busy teaching, it takes away from my writing time. Conversely, when I'm teaching, I'm excited about writing, and I make the most of the free time that I *do* have.

I'm going to avoid becoming tedious here. You either want the teaching experience—or rather, the experience of teaching—or you want the time. I'm ranking teaching third. Consider it in your own way, and rank it accordingly.

We sense that you want to get off this subject, but at the same time, you don't *really* want to get off this subject.

Ah, you are the masters of intuition and observation. You will make wonderful writers.

Keep in mind: Some programs will want you to teach from the first semester forward. Others, the second year. Meanwhile, some programs would like you to teach two or three classes a semester, and I would encourage you to stay *well away* from these programs. These graduate students are more indentured servants than writers in training.

I really think highly of teaching experience. I became a better writer in trying to improve the writing of others. Teaching brings me energy and insight, and if you feel like it will do the same for you, keep this aspect high on your list of criteria

Are there other types of assistantships?

Yes. There are also research assistantships, where you do, well, research on behalf of a professor on a particular topic. This can be very rewarding and can teach you a lot of skills. They also pay, usually quite well for the hours involved. Editorial assistantships are also often available if the university has a literary magazine or small press. These assistantships are, obviously, a great way to acquire editing experience.

Last thoughts on assistantships?

Be sure to find information about assistantships on the program's Web site. Often, the application for these positions is separate from the actual graduate application. Also often, they are required *after* you've been accepted, and not before.

So, decide whether or not you'll want to teach or research or not. Aim at programs that offer your preference. (And decide whether there are enough positions to go around. The Web site should indicate a number or a percentage.) Teaching is actually part of "funding," though teaching is more than funding, so I list it separately.

Can you summarize where we are right now?

These top three criteria—location, funding, and teaching—are the main criteria for most students, at least in their initial research stage. If you don't care where you live, and you don't need funding, and you don't care to teach, then you'll move the following criteria way up. Otherwise, you will have narrowed your search of hundreds of schools down to about twenty or thirty, or fewer in some cases, based on these top three criteria.

Okay, what's the fourth criteria?

Faculty is the fourth criteria.

Good teachers are happy with their jobs, they make themselves available to students, they run creative and supportive classes, and they have a keen eye for helping students shape and deepen their creative work. I'd say that the vast majority of writing instructors take their work in the classroom very seriously, and they enjoy the give-and-take of interacting with students. Good teachers are often good writers. They learn from their teaching and they learn from their students.

That said, I place "faculty" as number four in our criteria because it is not a certain or measurable aspect. As I said in the previous chapter, some professors are on sabbatical, others move from program to program, others are terrific writers but lousy teachers. A good faculty is steady, generous with their time, and productive as writers.

Much about faculty, at least in this early stage of your selection process, is the luck of the draw. Perhaps one of your main professors will be on sabbatical for your first year. And perhaps that professor will be replaced with a visiting writer who understands and encourages your work. Perhaps this substitute is just what you need for your writing.

My point? The faculty criteria is unpredictable. That said, take a look at the faculty of your potential programs. Are there writers here whom you admire? Are there writers whom you might admire if you knew their work? Well, find their work in bookstores, in libraries, or online. Read them. Is there someone whom you admire in particular, someone who writes similarly to you, or similarly to how you'd like to write? Great. By all means, move this program up in your rankings. But keep in mind: Someone who writes very differently from you may actually be a great help to you. You'll change as a writer as you move through a program. Keep faculty in mind, but keep them in perspective.

Don't you want to say something here about low-residency programs?

Yes. Faculty is going to matter much more in low-residency programs for three obvious reasons. First, location is not a priority since your location is where you're currently living. Second, funding is not a priority since low-residency programs offer few fellowships and scholarships. Third, your experience will be primarily with faculty, not with other students. Definitely narrow your choices, and then definitely read the work of the faculty on your list.

For more information about low-residency programs, see my interview with Scott McCabe in chapter 6.

What about program size?

It's possible that this might be a big priority for you. Some programs admit as few as a ten students; others admit fifty or more. Three thoughts come to my mind:

1. Programs that accept a large number of students are more likely to include *you* in that large number of students. In other words, if one program accepts thirty students and another only twelve, then just based on the law of averages, you're more likely to be accepted to the larger program. As you narrow your list, it may be wise to have a mix of smaller and larger programs.
2. Keep in mind that your experience in a creative writing program will rely in large part on your interactions with other graduate students writers. A larger program will feature more like-minded students and more not-like-minded students. Smaller programs, fewer for each. Consider the obvious question: Do you like smaller groups or larger ones?
3. Finally, generally speaking, smaller programs are better in the funding aspect. They have fewer students to fund, and so they push their resources to these students.

Can you list the remaining criteria in bullet-point form?

My thoughts exactly. Let's keep this bus moving.

- Perhaps you'd like to study in *more* than one genre (fiction, poetry, nonfiction, screenwriting, playwriting, children's fiction etc.) Some schools offer this option, but most don't. If you're interested in this option, adjust your rankings accordingly.

- Two years or more? Most M.F.A. programs are two years, though many are three-years. Many of the M.A. programs will be one year, and of course Ph.D. programs will be five years or more. The only thing I have to say about this is that I got most of my best writing done in the third year of my experience at the University of Massachusetts. How important is time to you? Do you have one or two years to devote to your craft, or do you have more? Adjust your rankings accordingly.
- Finally, do remember the other aspects of writing programs. Things like reading series, community outreach, and literary journals. It's my opinion that these aspects may be more important to you in the final selection process, and not as critical in this preliminary narrowing process. Sift your programs down to a dozen. Then apply. Then include these smaller though important criteria in your final selection process.

Chapter Summary

1. A solid graduate program in creative writing provides funding for the majority of its students, teaching experience, a well-regarded faculty, and good class sizes (10–12) and student to teacher ratio (12 to 1 or less). Literary magazines and presses are helpful to a program and its students, as is community outreach and an impressive visiting writers series. A graduate student reading series is a good sign of a solid program, as are a required thesis and student representation on planning committees. A course list with a variety of classes is a must, as is a little flexibility in taking classes outside the department. Contacts with editors and agents, a strong record of publication from past graduates, and a high graduation rate (85 percent or higher) are all signs of an impressive program.

2 You can find a lot of preliminary information on creative writing program Web sites. I've listed them in the back of this book. A poorly designed Web site often indicates a poorly designed program. Information about funding, faculty, and other criteria should be directly stated and easy to find.

3. Location should be your first criteria in selecting a program. Make sure you'll live in a place where you'll be comfortable and challenged. Aspects like big city vs. small college town, region of

the country, and cultural amenities are important factors in making your program experience a success.

4. Funding should be your second criteria. And it's a close second. Unless you're independently wealthy of course; then you've got lots of options. Seek programs that fund all or the majority of their graduate students. Avoid poorly funded programs. Keep in mind that programs that "tier" their students can sometimes create a competitive atmosphere. Seek funding and seek programs with affordable tuition. Information about funding should be clearly stated on the program Web site.

5. Teaching assistantships and fellowships are terrific ways to gain experience and improve your writing. They also provide funding, as do research and editorial assistantships. Avoid programs that offer *too much experience* (i.e., programs that require you to teach two or three classes a semester). A good program offers a good balance of experience and writing time.

6. The criteria in this chapter are for narrowing your schools and applying to those schools, not for making your final selection of where you want to attend. More on that in chapter 5.

7. A good faculty can make an enormously positive impact on your graduate experience. Possibly the most important impact. However, it's difficult to determine the level of teaching and availability of professors at this early stage. Leave that for your final selections. Do look at the faculty of your prospective schools, and do read their work. However, location, funding, and teaching experience are much more important at this early stage.

8. Faculty is more important for low-residency programs at this early stage, as location and funding are likely already determined.

9. Program size is important for reasons of community, funding, and acceptance rate. Applying to a mix of smaller and larger programs might be a good idea.

10. Other factors to consider: flexibility in classes and genre, reading series, and literary journals.

CHAPTER 3

The Programs

IN 1997, U.S. NEWS AND WORLD REPORTS set out to rank the top creative writing programs. They distributed a questionnaire to four members of each creative writing university—including deans, program directors, and professors—asking them to grade, on a scale of 5 (highest) to 1 (lowest), the other programs in the nation. Responders were asked not to grade programs that they had little knowledge of. The outcome, published in 1998 (and republished in 2002, but the same), was a listing of almost 100 programs, each ranging in grade from 4.5 to around 2.0. In many ways, this survey and its results have been a touchstone for prospective graduate students since that time.

And of course, it's become a subject of great and often heated debate within the writing community. My opinion is that the rankings are relatively fair and accurate. They judge the reputation of a program based on the strength of the faculty and the publishing and professional success of its students and former students. That said, the rankings are many years old now, and they *do not at all* reflect the top two criteria of this handbook: location and funding.

I can't much comment on location. You know what you need as far as where you'd like to live and work. In my comments below about the programs I may include a sentence or two about the particular community where a program resides. Any lack of a comment should indicate my lack of knowledge, rather than any judgment on my part.

Funding, however, I'll comment upon. As you've read before, I think it's very important for programs to fund their students, or, at the very least, for programs to make their tuition affordable. To my mind, the best programs fund all of their students and fund them all equally. Rank funding in your own criteria, and judge it accordingly.

Check it out: I'm not going to "rank" the programs in the traditional sense. Instead, I'm going to take fifty of the most recognized master's programs—new and old—and divide them into geographic areas of the United States. I'll note top five, ten, or twenty when a program is particularly distinguished. I'm not as familiar with low-residency and Ph.D. programs as I am with resident master's programs, so I'll simply point out the most recognized programs in these two areas.

I want you to think about these comments as a *starting* point, not an ending point. Look out, here comes the bus driver metaphor again: You've just arrived in a city. The city of graduate writing programs, and I'm the bus driver, giving you a brief tour. Just because I pass a street without comment doesn't mean it's not worth your time to explore it. That may end up being the best street for you. I'm giving you an overview. I encourage and expect you to branch out from here, using the profiles at the back of the book for your door-by-door experience. If you stick to these fifty listings, then you may have an outstanding graduate experience. If not, then I'd not be surprised, and don't go blaming the bus driver. Do explore programs that I have not profiled in this chapter.

This chapter is going to make me very unpopular in the writing community. Writers have very strong feelings about their programs. However, that's my problem, not yours. My intention is to be accurate and fair, but not diplomatic. This guide is a friend of the prospective student, not of the individual programs. Basically, what I say in the profiles is what I say to my students who are interested in particular programs. I'm basing my judgments on the same criteria we spoke about in chapter 2, with the exception of location. Of course, I'll definitely indicate the three universities that I attended during undergraduate, graduate, and postgraduate education.

New England

Boston University—A one-year M.A. program in fiction, poetry, and playwriting . . . eight classes (four workshops, three English graduate courses, and one course with flexibility) and a creative thesis. Students may take one workshop in another genre . . . Twelve fiction writers, twelve poets, and six playwrights are accepted . . . There are teaching fellowships available, and a couple of writing fellowships, but the teaching fellowships offer only partial tuition relief (half to three-quarters), and this is a private university with a high tuition. It seems that the average student receives half funding . . . A very impressive faculty . . . The playwriting program is part of the Boston Playwrights Theatre . . . The program includes a lot of interesting classes, good attention from faculty, but, it seems, not much free time to write, as students take four classes a semester . . . The Boston University program has always been held in very high regard. I do worry about the high tuition.

Brown University—A two-year M.F.A. program in fiction, poetry, playwriting, and one spot in electronic writing. In Providence, RI . . . Eight classes total. Four workshops and four classes that can be *any* class offered at the university. Highly unusual and, I think, impressive . . . A program that provides a great deal of writing time . . . Brown is known as a program that favors "experimental" writing. What exactly does that mean? Hard to say. If you write nontraditional narratives and poetry, then this might be a good program to take a look at . . . The campus is quite beautiful . . . The program seems to work hard to provide financial assistance to all of its students . . . An outstanding faculty . . . This program is highly selective. They take about fourteen students out of seven hundred applicants . . . Thought of as the most important writing program in the experimental field. A top-twenty program overall.

Emerson College—A two- to three-year M.F.A. program in fiction, poetry, nonfiction, screenwriting, and children's literature. In Boston, MA . . . The program also includes an interesting M.A. degree in publishing and writing for students looking to work in the editing and publishing industry . . . The funding here looks very poor, with a very small salary for those who receive teaching assistantships, especially considering the cost of living in Boston. Otherwise, very little funding . . . *Ploughshares*, an excellent literary magazine, is based at Emerson . . . There are a number of interesting classes here, but there doesn't seem to be much support for graduate students, especially considering the cost of living in Boston and the tuition of a private university . . . This program seems underfunded and overrated.

University of Massachusetts—A three-year program in fiction and poetry in Amherst, MA . . . This is where I did my M.F.A . . . Sixteen courses total, with four workshops, six literature or craft courses, and some flexibility with the final two classes. A creative thesis and defense is also required . . . An innovative Five-College Program, where students may take classes at neighboring Smith College, Mount Holyoke, Amherst, or Hampshire College . . . The program receives many applications and accepts a high number of students (around 25 or more) . . . Teaching experience is very good here, and funding is available to almost all students. Research and work-study positions are also available . . . Amherst is a beautiful college town, as is neighboring Northampton . . . The literary magazines *jubilat* and *The Massachusetts Review* are part of the writing program . . . I liked it at UMass Amherst, very much, and would definitely recommend the experience . . . Easily a top-twenty program.

University of New Hampshire—A two year M.A. program in fiction, nonfiction, and poetry in Durham, NH . . . This is a two-year master's of English with a writing option . . . Around fifteen to twenty students accepted a year . . . Only two workshops required, as opposed to the usual four for a two-year program. Eight classes total, two workshops and six English literature courses . . . Some teaching assistantships are available, but I would call this about middle-of-the-road as far as funding goes . . . Durham, NH, is a nice town, and cold, cold in the winter. A good opportunity to write during those months . . . This is a literature degree with a writing component, not the other way around . . . A solid program for funded students.

New York City and State

Brooklyn College—A two-year M.F.A. program in fiction, poetry, and playwriting. In Brooklyn, NYC . . . Nine classes total, including four workshops, four literature courses, two reading seminars, and two one-on-one tutorials with professors. The reading seminars and especially the one-on-one tutorials are innovative and impressive. . . . The faculty to student ratio is very good . . . Some students are funded through scholarships, teaching assistantships, and otherwise. Middle-of-the-road as far as funding goes, but the sense is that it is improving here, and that faculty and administration actively seek it for their students. . . . There is some flexibility in taking classes outside the department . . . This program actually posts the e-mails of many of their students on the Web site, so you can ask them questions directly. I've never seen this before, and it says to me that there is a strong relationship between faculty and students. . . . I think this is an up-and-coming program, and if you like New York City, don't fail to check this program out.

Columbia University—A two- to three-year M.F.A. program in fiction, poetry, and nonfiction in New York City . . . The CU Web site is extremely confusing about class requirements. My best guess: sixteen classes, with four workshops and the remaining literature classes, writing seminars, and electives . . . Many recent graduates of the program have published books and secured positions at universities and publishing houses . . . Columbia is *expensive*. And the financial aid isn't very impressive. Any time students are referred to the Office of Student Affairs, you know you're not going to get much financial support from the program. A small number of teaching assistantships are available in the second year to qualified applicants . . . There seems to be a very interesting affiliation with local public schools to bring writers and artists into the classroom . . . A highly regarded faculty . . . They accept a very large number of students. Around seventy a year . . . If you can afford it, go for it. If not, there are equally good programs out there for much less money.

Cornell University—A two-year M.F.A. program in poetry and fiction in Ithaca, NY . . . Ten classes total, including four workshops, four literature classes, and two electives . . . A very small two-year program. Only four poets and four fiction writers are accepted each year . . . As you might expect, a very good faculty to student ratio . . . Outstanding funding. All students are funded through teaching assistantships and editorial internships with the highly regarded *Epoch* literary magazine. . . . Ithaca is a nice college town. Very chilly winters, relatively mild summers . . . The program also offers teaching opportunities to graduates of the program for up to two years . . . This is a difficult program to be accepted into, but it has a strong emphasis on teaching, editing, and, of course, writing . . . I think very highly of this program. One of the best in the nation, and easily in the top ten.

New York University—A two-year M.F.A. in creative writing and a two-year M.A. in English with a concentration in creative writing. In fiction and poetry in New York City . . . Four workshops and four literature classes, plus the creative thesis . . . The program may be taken part-time for up to five years . . . An outstanding permanent and visiting faculty. Lots of variety . . . Around two-thirds of students receive partial fellowships in teaching, community outreach, and writing, and a few students receive full funding. . . . The program seems to be *very* involved in the community. There is a terrific literary outreach program . . . This is one of the top twenty programs in the country. I'd like the funding to be better. Especially attractive for those receiving fellowships.

Sarah Lawrence College—A two-year M.F.A. program in poetry, fiction, and nonfiction writers in Bronxville, NY . . . Students may also attend the program part-time . . . Four workshops and four to five additional classes in craft, thesis, and electives . . . Offers impressive biweekly one-on-one conferences with professors . . . An interesting Community-of-Writers program offers outreach to a variety of community organizations . . . Students may volunteer with *Lumina*, the literary magazine connected with the program . . . Very little funding available to graduate students. A very few students receive funding through the college . . . A highly regarded faculty . . . A beautiful campus . . . A solid program, but the funding situation and the high tuition may be a serious concern for prospective students.

Syracuse University—A three-year M.F.A. program in fiction and poetry. Highly selective: accepts only six students in each genre per year. Outstanding faculty-to-student ratio; one of the best in the country . . . Workshops are taken only in the fall, and the 48 credit hour degree includes classes in form and style, literature classes within the department, and good flexibility in taking classes outside the department. I like this structure. Seems very innovative to me . . . Funding is very good. All students receive full funding . . . There are a good number of teaching assistantships available . . . An impressive faculty. Sort of a young faculty for whatever that's worth . . . Former students are very enthusiastic about this program . . . A very strong program, right up there with the best on the national level. Easily in the top ten.

The Mid-Atlantic Coast

George Mason University—A three-year M.F.A. program in fiction, poetry, and creative nonfiction in Fairfax, VA . . . 48 semester hours, including at least four in writing seminars, four classes in literature, and the remaining in electives and thesis work. There is also a written examination required . . . Thirty-eight students accepted each year . . . There are certainly a variety of funding sources available in assistantships and fellowships, but the quantity of funding sources is in the middle-of-the-road category . . . George Mason is located fifteen miles outside Washington, DC . . . This is a solid program with a very fine reputation. Especially attractive for funded students.

Hollins College—A two- to three-year M.F.A. program in poetry, fiction, and creative nonfiction in Roanoke, VA . . . A 48 degree hour program. Ten classes, plus the thesis. "Courses may be in the immediate area of the degree, or, if the student's background and preparation warrant, in related areas. At least one course each term must be a literature course which includes a substantial critical paper." . . . Funding is above average. "Stipends and scholarships are available to qualified students." . . . Graduates of the Hollins program have had great success in getting their work published . . . A relatively young faculty . . . The Hollins program has always been held in high regard, and is a definite consideration for any prospective student.

Johns Hopkins University—A two-year program that has just changed from a long-running M.A. program to a new M.F.A. program (though the M.A. program is still available. See below) . . . Fiction or poetry concentrations in Baltimore, MD . . . Four workshops, four literature or craft courses, plus the creative thesis . . . Approximately five poets and six fiction writers are admitted annually . . . Students are fully funded in the form of teaching assistantships. This is great, though keep in mind that teaching is a requirement, not an option . . . Students must turn in half of their thesis after one year. I think this is impressive. It says that the faculty wants to be involved and helpful during the entire process, not just at the end. . . . There is a secondary language requirement . . . This program has always been thought of highly in the writing community. The M.F.A. program is an excellent addition. One of the top ten programs in the country . . . There is also a continuation of the long-running M.A. program in creative writing, though this program focuses on part-time students, and if that's what you're looking for, this would be an excellent option for you . . . Additionally, there is an M.A. in science writing.

Penn State University—A three-year M.F.A. program in poetry, fiction, and creative nonfiction in University Park, PA . . . A 48 degree hour program, including five workshops, five literature courses, two electives, and a final writing project . . . Around twelve students accepted each year . . . All students are funded in the form of teaching assistantships, though students will teach two classes some semesters . . . Former students have a good publication track record . . . A good student to faculty ratio of about 3 to 1 . . . A good program, though the teaching load is a concern.

University of Maryland—A two-year program in fiction and poetry in College Park, MD . . . Four workshop courses, four literature courses, one outside the department, and one craft and form course . . . An outstanding faculty. I mean, *really* outstanding. Former students often rave about their availability, knowledge, and enthusiasm . . . Recent graduates have shown some impressive publishing success . . . Funding is less than average, though definitely present in the form of a few fellowships and a few teaching assistantships . . . This program has a very good reputation, especially in the last decade. The funding is a concern for some prospective students, though in-state funding is reasonable. A very good addition to any prospective student's list.

University of North Carolina Greensboro—A two-year program in fiction and poetry in Greensboro, NC . . . This is where I did my undergraduate work . . . 36 degree hours total. Classes include up to four workshops, four craft and literature classes, and a very interesting editing sequence of courses that gives students hands-on experience through the literary journal, *The Greensboro Review*, and other places. There are also one-on-one tutorials and some flexibility for outside-the-department courses . . . Ten to twelve students admitted each year . . . More than half of students receive full funding in the form of teaching and research assistantships, and it seems that the remaining students normally receive some form of funding . . . This was the first exposure I'd ever had to a graduate writing program. Years later, I am still surprised at how many other programs fall short in the attention and care that faculty show toward their students. This is a small program, one with an excellent teacher-to-student ratio, and would be a good fit for prospective students interested in mentoring and one-on-one attention . . . A consistently solid program with an impressive faculty.

University of North Carolina Wilmington—A three-year program in fiction, poetry, and creative nonfiction in the coastal town of Wilmington, NC . . . 48 degree hours total, which breaks down to about five writing classes, six to seven literature courses, and six hours of thesis credit . . . An M.F.A. exam and thesis is also required . . . Has an interesting publishing laboratory that offers experience in editing, design, production, and marketing . . . I like this program. It's relatively new, and certainly very innovative . . . The program is connected to but officially separate from the English department. This is unusual and quite possibly a good thing . . . Students may explore a minor concentration in screenwriting through the Department of Film Studies . . . About a third of students are awarded teaching assistantships, and other students receive partial funding . . . About 15–20 students accepted per year . . . I'd like the funding to be better, but overall this is an up-and-coming writing program.

University of Pittsburgh—A three-year M.F.A. in fiction, poetry, and creative nonfiction in Pittsburgh, PA . . . U of Pitt is one of the oldest writing programs in the country and was one of the first to offer nonfiction in the degree . . . Around twenty-one students are admitted each year . . . Courseload is 36 hours total, with three workshops and the remaining classes in the English or foreign language departments (though there is no foreign language requirement) . . . Creative nonfiction requirements provide flexibility in out-of-department classes . . . The University of Pittsburgh Press, which runs the Drue Heinz Literature Prize, is associated with the program . . . Funding seems about middle-of-the-road, "to a few qualified entering students in the form of Teaching Assistantships and Graduate Student Assistantships.". . . . This has always been a well-regarded program. I'd like the funding to be better.

University of Virginia—A small, two-year M.F.A. program in Charlottesville, VA . . . Admits five poets and seven fiction writers per year . . . Requirements are four workshops and four literature courses, plus a creative manuscript and an oral exam . . . An outstanding faculty . . . Holds one of the best literary libraries in the country . . . Recent grads have had very good publication success. . . . All students are funded. . . . Charlottesville is your typical college town. If you're looking for the big city, this isn't it . . . The lit magazine *Meridian* is run by the program . . . Former students are very enthusiastic about this program. This is one of the top ten programs in the country.

The Southeast

Florida State University—A two-year M.A. program in literature with an emphasis in creative writing in Tallahassee, FL . . . Poetry, fiction, essay, and drama writing . . . Nine classes total, with four workshops and five literature classes . . . Financial support seems quite good, with the majority of students receiving teaching assistantships . . . Has an interesting editing and publishing program related to the degree, as well as a graduate teacher training program . . . *The Southeast Review* is connected to the department . . . A very impressive faculty . . . This program, as the degree indicates, leans more toward the literature component than an M.F.A. program would . . . A solid program with a very good reputation. . . . *Note: Florida State plans to add an M.F.A. degree in the very near future.*

University of Alabama—A longer M.F.A. program (three to four years) in Tuscaloosa, AL . . . Poetry or fiction concentrations, with secondary studies in digital media, nonfiction, autobiography, and screenwriting . . . Fourteen classes total, including five workshops, three "forms" classes (literature classes aimed at writers), one class in "writers at work," four literature classes, one elective class . . . 48 hours total, plus a thesis . . . This program, while longer, offers great flexibility of class choice and concentration . . . Support is impressive: "It's our policy to accept only applicants to whom we can pledge financial support for the duration of their programs." . . . Many teaching assistantships available . . . *The Black Warrior Review* is based within the program . . . Around twelve to fifteen students are accepted each year . . . An impressive and innovative program. On the rise.

University of Arkansas—A three-year program in fiction, poetry, or translation in Fayetteville, AR . . . 60 hours of coursework (around eighteen classes total), divided between workshops, writing technique courses, and literature courses . . . Students may also take classes in screenwriting and creative nonfiction . . . The program is associated with the Writers in Schools Project, visiting local high schools to conduct workshops . . . Funding seems middle-of-the-road, with teaching assistantships and writing fellowships available to some students . . . Former students have a good publication track record . . . The faculty is impressive . . . Twelve to fifteen students accepted per year . . . A program with a good reputation. A very good choice for students who receive funding, and tuition is affordable for those who do not.

University of Florida—An intensive two-year program in poetry and fiction in Gainesville, FL . . . Four workshops, three literature classes, three one-on-one reading tutorials, a thesis, and some flexibility with two electives . . . I like the availability of the reading tutorials. It says much about this program . . . I would call the funding here above average to good, with a concentration on teaching assistantships . . . Former students have had good success in the publication and professional world . . . Eight permanent faculty members, all impressive . . . This is one of the oldest programs in the country, is very highly regarded, and should be considered strongly by any prospective student.

University of Georgia—An M.A. in English with a creative writing thesis, in one of my favorite college towns, Athens, GA . . . Poetry, fiction, or creative nonfiction . . . The M.A. is two years and twelve classes. There are two "writing seminars" instead of workshops, and the remaining ten classes are in literature . . . This program concentrates on literature studies first and creative writing second . . . The poetry journal *Verse* is associated with the program, as is the literary magazine *The Georgia Review* (some students may intern with one or the other) . . . Some students are funded their first year (research assistantships) and all students are offered teaching assistantships in their second year. This is above-average funding . . . The Web site does a nice job of explaining the overall course of study . . . A very good program for students wanting to concentrate in literature studies with a lesser though still important concentration in creative writing.

Louisiana State University—A three-year M.F.A. program in fiction, poetry, drama, and screenwriting in Baton Rouge, LA . . . There are also workshops available in literary nonfiction and translation . . . 48 degree hours, with five workshops, including one in another genre, five literature courses, and three electives . . . Funding seems above average, with teaching fellowships, tuition waivers, and supplemental funding available to some students, and editorial experience is available with up to three literary journals . . . A very good student-to-teacher ratio . . . The program's Web site was one of the best I visited, and it encourages students to contact the program director with any questions . . . This program seems to have flown a bit under the radar up till now. I'm not sure why that is. A very strong program, and a worthy addition to any prospective student's list.

University of Mississippi—A three-year M.F.A. program in fiction and poetry in Oxford, MS . . . This is a relatively new program, and is highly selective. The program accepts three to five students total a year . . . 42 degree hours, including four workshops, five literature courses, three electives, and the rest thesis credit. The program does require a foreign language proficiency, a book list, and a comprehensive final exam . . . Funding seems very good, with full writing and teaching fellowships available to most students . . . The program has an innovative community outreach series featuring readings, tutoring, and teaching . . . I think very highly of the faculty at Mississippi. Outstanding writers, outstanding teachers . . . This program seems to have a clear vision for mentoring and encouraging its new writers . . . One of the up-and-comers. A very impressive program.

The Midwest

Indiana University—A three-year M.F.A. program in fiction and poetry in Bloomington, IN. IU also offers a two-year M.A. program. . . . Six M.F.A. fiction students admitted each year, and six in poetry . . . The M.F.A. is a 60-hour degree, with four workshops, five or more literature classes, and some flexibility in taking courses outside the department . . . The M.A. degree is 30 hours, with two workshops, five literature courses, and flexibility with one course . . . All students receive funding in the form of teaching assistantships and/or supplemental fellowships . . . This program pays close attention to diversity resources and has specific funding for minority students . . . *The Indiana Review* is run by graduate students . . . Former students have a good track record in publishing and teaching . . . In general, there is excellent support and interest from the program in its students . . . Also offers class credit for work in playwriting, screenwriting, and translation . . . Bloomington is a great college town . . . Eleven faculty members. That's a lot, and that's good . . . This program was already highly regarded. That said, it's my opinion that it's not regarded enough. From a prospective student's point of view, or anyone's point of view for that matter, this is one of the top programs in the country. Easily in the top five.

Iowa State University—A one-to two-year M.A. in English, specialization in creative writing, in Ames, IA . . . Poetry and fiction . . . Unlike some other M.A. degrees, Iowa State's program definitely emphasizes the creative writing aspect . . . 30 degree hours including four writing classes, two literature, and three electives . . . Funding looks about average to above in the areas of teaching and research assistantships. The English department seems to work hard to find funding for its students . . . Not much other information available on this program . . . What can I say? What's available looks good. Otherwise, a little mysterious.

University of Iowa—A two-year M.F.A. program in fiction, poetry, and nonfiction in Iowa City . . . Known as The Writers Workshop, the program is the oldest in the country, and is often regarded as the best . . . I guess you could say that graduates have had some publishing success. As in, say, a dozen Pulitzer Prizes. Four recent U.S. poet laureates are graduates of the program. Many, many, many have had success in the publishing and professional world . . . The program has been the model for other programs for decades . . . Iowa City is a terrific college town . . . The Nonfiction Writers Program is separate from the Writers Workshop . . . More than sixty students are admitted each year . . . 48 semester hours: half in writing workshops and classes, and the rest with great flexibility to take classes in or outside the department . . . Funding is available, but very competitive. The top third of students receive full funding, the middle third receive full to some funding, the bottom third receive some to no funding. In-state tuition is affordable . . . This "tiered" system of funding sets up a very competitive atmosphere within the program. Students are in competition with each other for funding before they enter the program and, for some, after the first year . . . A very distinguished faculty . . . To be fair, because The Iowa Writers Workshop is so highly regarded, it creates a lot of supporters and many detractors . . . I don't like the competitive funding system, though this is not unique to Iowa . . . What I can tell you is this: the Iowa graduates that I have met are either very enthusiastic about the program, or very down on it. Rarely do I meet someone in the middle. My sense is that their reactions are often related to their funding or lack of it, and how they were treated within the program accordingly . . . Because of the funding situation, Iowa is no longer the best program in the country, and because of the competitive atmosphere, it should not be considered a top-ten program either . . . This program should be considered by any prospective student, especially those who are awarded funding. A top-twenty program.

University of Michigan—A two-year M.F.A. program in fiction or poetry in Ann Arbor, MI . . . A 36 hour degree program, with four workshops, four literature courses, a thesis, and a secondary language requirement. There is some flexibility in taking courses outside the department . . . Funding is excellent, mostly arriving in the form of teaching assignments . . . In addition, the program "sponsors a number of colloquia each year on such topics as commercial publishing, freelance book reviewing, government grants for writers in the schools, volunteer work in the arts, and community outreach." I really like this aspect . . . Ann Arbor is a typical and likeable college town. Man, it gets cold in the winter, though. A good time for writing . . . Around twenty students are accepted each year . . . An outstanding faculty . . . Michigan has long been considered one of the top programs in the country in creative writing. It belongs on any prospective student's list. A top-five program.

University of Minnesota—A three-year M.F.A. program in fiction, poetry, and nonfiction in Minneapolis, MN . . . The program is "committed to providing financial support for students for three full years." That's terrific . . . Around fifteen students accepted per year. . . . The requirements seem innovative and well-rounded. They included four workshops, three literature courses, two courses in a related field (studio art, secondary language, editing, history, music, dance, etc.) a reading list, an M.F.A. essay, and the creative thesis . . . An outstanding faculty . . . Recent former students have had good publishing success . . . There seems to be a priority on community outreach through school-age mentoring, Web projects, and readings in the community . . . This is a program ranked low on the *U.S. News* list, and that's either a mistake or the program has come a long way in a short time. Minnesota is an impressive program and is worthy of strong consideration by prospective students. A worthy addition to anyone's list.

Notre Dame University—A two-year M.F.A. program in poetry, fiction and nonfiction in South Bend, IN . . . three workshops, four literature courses, and the rest in thesis preparation . . . Ten total students admitted per year . . . All accepted students receive full tuition waivers, and some students receive additional teaching and writing fellowships. That's impressive . . . Students can work on the *Notre Dame Review*, a national literary journal . . . Former students have had good publishing success . . . This is a solid program and seems to be on the rise.

University of Cincinnati—A two- to three-year M.A. program in poetry and fiction in Cincinnati, OH . . . A 54 degree hour program. The Web site is confusing about the distribution of these hours. My best guess: five workshops, two graduate research classes, plus six literature classes, a three-part M.A. exam, and the thesis. This is a lot of work for an M.A. degree. Students are definitely immersed in literature . . . Has a very interesting professional writing and editing course of study . . . The number of teaching assistantships "varies" from year to year, but I'd grade funding here as about average . . . This is a program to consider for students who wish to concentrate in literature.

University of Wisconsin Madison—A two-year M.F.A. program in fiction and poetry, in Madison, WI . . . Admissions is a little unusual here, as fiction writers apply in odd-numbered years, poets in even-numbered years, and applications are due in December. Six students accepted annually . . . All students are funded with teaching assistantships . . . 36 degree hours, with three workshops, three electives, and the rest thesis hours . . . An outstanding faculty . . . In the great college town of Madison, WI . . . Students I've spoken to were enthusiastic about this program . . . This program was not ranked in the *U.S. News and World Report* rankings. Not sure why that is. An impressive program, and a worthy addition to any student's list. . . . *Also, the Wisconsin Institute for Creative Writing provides $25,000 resident fellowships for students who have completed an M.F.A. or Ph.D. at any school. Six writers are annually chosen.*

Washington University, Missouri—A two-year M.F.A. program in fiction or poetry in St. Louis, MO. . . . Great flexibility here. Four workshops, a creative thesis, and eight "graduate-level academic courses selected in consultation with the Director of the Program from any department in which the student has the appropriate preparation and whose graduate offerings can enrich the student's writing." I like this . . . This is a small program, only admitting around eight students a year . . . Funding is excellent, generally consisting of tuition scholarships and fellowship stipends in the first year, and teaching assistantships in the second year . . . The faculty is very good, and there is also an impressive visiting faculty program . . . If you like small programs and excellent coursework flexibility, then Washington University should top your list. Has long been known as an outstanding program. One of the top twenty in the nation.

The Southwest

Arizona State University—A two- to three-year M.F.A. program in fiction, poetry, or screenwriting in Tempe, AZ . . . The 48 degree hour program in fiction and poetry is split 24/24 between writing and literature classes . . . The screenwriting degree is 60 hours, and students actually work *in* the theater department in collaboration with actors and directors . . . Funding is definitely "tiered" here, with some students receiving teaching and research assistantships, and others receiving nothing. That said, there seems to be good effort to get students in-state tuition and even tuition waivers through university work. I'd list funding as average. . . . There is interesting community outreach through the Young Writers at Work and the Reach Out programs . . . This is a very large program, with about twenty-five students accepted each year . . . I think very highly of this faculty, and word from previous students is that they show a great interest in student work and learning . . . I'd like the funding to be better, of course, and I'm concerned about the competition that the tiered system creates. That said, this is a solid M.F.A. program, with good innovation within the genres. Historically, the ASU program has been highly regarded.

University of Arizona—A two-year M.F.A. program in fiction, poetry, and creative nonfiction in Tucson, AZ . . . Twelve classes total, including four workshops, two craft seminars, six electives in English or other departments, and a creative thesis. I like the flexibility here . . . This is a very large program, with more than twenty-five students accepted per year . . . Funding is below average, with a little less than half of students receiving funding in the form of teaching assistantships or writing fellowships. This sets up a competitive, tiered-funding situation. In-state tuition is affordable . . . Former students have a good record of publishing . . . An impressive Poetry Center, offering special collections and readings, is connected with the program . . . You can make a lot of this program if you receive funding. That said, keep your options open by also applying to schools with better funding . . . A distinguished program, but one that is no longer among the elite.

University of Houston—A two-year M.F.A. program in fiction or poetry in Houston, TX . . . Five workshops, five literature courses, and a creative thesis. Interestingly, fiction and poetry students must take one workshop in the other genre, so if you're interested in versatility, this is a good program to look at . . . Twenty students admitted each year, ten in each genre . . . Funding is outstanding. All students are funded, and most work in teaching assistantships . . . One of the best faculties in the country . . . Community outreach through the Writers in Schools project . . . Former students have had excellent publication success . . . Students can gain editorial experience through the national literary journal *Gulf Coast* . . . One of the top ten programs in the country.

University of Texas—A three-year M.F.A. program (known as the James Michener Center for Writers) in fiction, poetry, playwriting, and screenwriting. (There is also a two-year M.A. program in poetry or fiction, which has a strong literature component. Profile below.) In Austin, TX . . . Students in the M.F.A. program concentrate in two genres . . . Austin, TX, is one of the best cities in the country, with perhaps the best music scene and a lively community of art and theater . . . A large and distinguished faculty. The student-to-teacher ratio is outstanding . . . Highly selective. Twelve students accepted per year . . . All students are fully funded. One of the best financial packages in the country. No teaching assistantships: This means, 1. Students have a lot of time to write, and 2. They don't gain much teaching experience. (However, there is a very interesting Writer's Outreach Program, where M.F.A. students teach courses in the community.) This will appeal to many prospective students and not to others . . . The coursework is very different from other programs, and it provides excellent flexibility: a first-year seminar, five workshops in primary and secondary fields, four courses in primary and secondary fields, four electives, and a creative thesis . . . I think the world of this program. Very innovative. Very supportive of its students . . . Because the program was founded in 1993, its ranking in the 1997 *U.S. News* ranking was #32. A huge mistake . . . This program is easily in the top five in the country.

University of Texas—A two-year M.A. program in poetry or fiction in Austin, TX . . . Course requirements in both literature and creative writing . . . There is a secondary language requirement, and graduate students can work as teaching assistants . . . Full funding . . . My sense is that this is an excellent program for students who wish a strong literature component to pair with the creative writing resources of the James Michener Center for Writers (above).

Texas State University—A three-year M.F.A. program in fiction and poetry, in San Marcos, TX . . . 48 degree hours, including four workshops, seven literature courses, and three electives . . . Enrolls around fifty-five students, with around 80 percent of them funded through teaching assistantships and other means . . . Very close attention to the final thesis here, with additional help from adjunct faculty . . . An impressive faculty . . . An innovative Young Writers Program, where M.F.A. students teach high school students during the summer . . . Definitely a program on the rise. Lots to like here.

The West

Colorado State University—A three-year M.F.A. program in fiction and poetry in Fort Collins, CO . . . 48 degree hours, including four workshops, two literature courses, one elective, and, interestingly, 12 degree hours devoted to the thesis. This is about double the degree hours for the thesis and indicates that a good amount of time is devoted to the finished work. A portfolio which includes an annotated bibliography of fifty works that were influential to the student is also required . . . Funding seems to be average, with many students working as teaching assistants . . . The literary magazines *Colorado Review* and *A* are associated with the program . . . Students have created a nice M.F.A. Survival Guide on the Web site . . . A good program, especially for funded students.

University of Nevada Las Vegas—A three-year M.F.A. program in fiction and poetry in Las Vegas, NV . . . This is definitely one of the most innovative programs in the country. Its requirements include study abroad, with an option with the Peace Corps . . . 54 degree hours total, with four workshops and eight literature courses. There is a focus on world literature here . . . Funding is very good, with students supported through teaching assistantships and other means . . . UNLV is also home to the International Institute of Modern Letters, a distinguished Ph.D. program in literature and creative writing, and City of Asylum, which provides sanctuary for writers fleeing political repression . . . I like what I see and hear about this program. Should be a top choice for anyone wishing to focus on travel, international studies, and world literature. The program is actually called M.F.A. in Creative Writing International. A top-twenty program.

University of Utah—A two-year M.F.A. program in poetry, fiction, nonfiction, and drama in Salt Lake City, UT . . . 33 degree hours, with four workshops and five literature courses, plus the creative thesis and an M.F.A. exam . . . Teaching assistantships are available, and I'd name the funding as average . . . I've heard good things, but the program also seems a little mysterious (in no small part due to its Web site). I'm wondering whether the M.F.A. students take a backseat to the Ph.D. students. . . . Worth a look into for prospective students.

Stanford University—The Stegner Fellowship program is a two-year non-degree program in fiction or poetry, and is often thought of as a post-M.F.A. program. Students without master's degrees have been accepted, though the main pool of applicants are students who are completing their graduate work . . . I was a Stegner Fellow during 2001–03 . . . "Stegners" take six workshops on the quarter system in two years, and they can also take almost any other course offered at Stanford . . . The fellowship offers that greatest of gifts: time. Time to write and complete a book or manuscript . . . Stanford is in Palo Alto, CA, though many fellows live in San Francisco and other Bay Area cities . . . Fully funded, with the additional opportunity for teaching assistantships in English department classes . . . Highly selective. Five poets and five fiction writers are selected from a pool of more than 1,200. . . . I loved my time at Stanford, and I'd highly recommend the Stegner program to advanced writers.

University of California Irvine—A two-year M.F.A. program in poetry or fiction in Irvine, CA . . . Twelve courses on the quarter system, half writing workshops, half literature courses. A thesis is also required . . . A small program. About ten to twelve students admitted per year . . . All students are funded in the form of fellowships and teaching assistantships, and all students will teach at some point during their stay . . . No program has a better publication track record by students than UC-Irvine in the last ten to fifteen years . . . An outstanding faculty . . . Grumble, grumble. The Web site leaves something to be desired, but don't hold that too much against them. This is one of the top five programs in the country, and quite possibly the best.

University of California Davis—A two-year M.A. program in fiction, nonfiction, or poetry . . . A 36 degree hour program, with four workshops, four literature courses, plus thesis hours . . . There is very good funding here, and a wide variety of choices for teaching assistance or on-campus work . . . Davis is a beautiful campus, and if you're looking for outdoor activities, this is a good place . . . A good faculty-to-student ratio . . . Students have good choices as far as out-of-department electives . . . This is a program that has flown under the radar up till now, but I expect that to change.

University of Montana—A two-year M.F.A. program in poetry and fiction in Missoula, MT . . . A 45 degree hour program, with four workshops, five classes in literature or craft, four classes outside the department (excellent flexibility), and 12 hours devoted to the thesis (meaning that the thesis is priority) . . . Around twenty to twenty five students accepted a year, so this is a large program . . . About half the students are funded in the form of teaching assistantships, so there is a tiered funding system . . . Former students have had good publishing success . . . *CutBank*, a literary journal, is associated with the program . . . A program held in high regard, though the competitive funding situation is an issue. That said, students who receive an offer of funding should strongly consider Montana.

The Pacific Northwest

Eastern Washington University—A two-year M.F.A. program in fiction, literary nonfiction, or poetry in Spokane, WA . . . A 72 degree hour program, though that is misleading. Each class counts as five credits. Four workshop, including one outside the concentration, four literature classes, three to five classes in electives, and a creative thesis . . . Between twenty and thirty students are admitted each year . . . Funding is below average. About eight incoming students are awarded two-year teaching assistantships. Second-year students may be awarded graduate assistantships . . . The literary journal *Willow Springs* is associated with the program . . . This is a program that seems to try hard, but is limited by a lack of funding. Is worthwhile to investigate if you want to live in this area of the country. Former students I've spoken with enjoyed their experience at EWU.

University of Oregon—A two-year M.F.A. program in fiction and poetry in Eugene, OR . . . A 72 degree hour program. Each class counts six credits, and the school is on the quarter system. Six workshops, three literature and craft courses, and the remaining credits in thesis preparation. Also, an M.F.A. examination. This program seems to be separate from the English department and definitely does not resemble an M.A. in English. The emphasis is on writing and craft . . . Around a dozen students are admitted each year . . . Eugene, OR, is a beautiful college town near the coast. Bring your raingear though . . . Graduates of the program have had excellent success in the publishing world . . . Funding is very good. At least 75 percent of students hold teaching fellowships . . . Some graduate students teach in the Kidd Tutorials, a one-year intensive creative writing course for undergraduates . . . Much to like here, including a very solid faculty. This is a top-twenty M.F.A. program.

University of Washington—A two-year M.F.A. program in poetry and fiction in Seattle, WA . . . 55 degree hours, a creative manuscript, a critical essay, and proficiency in a secondary language. Degree hours include four workshops, three literature classes, one elective, and the rest thesis credits . . . Around fifteen to twenty students accepted per year . . . Funding is available to some but definitely not all students. There is definitely a tiered system here. There are a few grants available, and M.F.A. students are eligible for work-study assistantships in other areas of the university. Bottom line: The funding here is average . . . The program is associated with the Writers in Schools program as well as the literary journal *The Seattle Review* . . . The faculty is as good as any in the country . . . Seattle has a rich literary tradition and is a great city . . . Students seem very involved with this program, even running the visiting writers series . . . I think highly of this program, as do most writers and teachers. I'm concerned about the tiered funding though. A good addition to prospective students' lists.

Ph.D. Programs

A complete listing of Ph.D. programs in creative writing or in English with concentrations in creative writing are available in Appendix D. Some of the more distinguished Ph.D. programs include the University of Southern California, the University of Houston, University of Missouri Columbia, University of Utah, Florida State University, Cornell University, and the University of Nevada Las Vegas.

Low-residency Programs

A complete listing of low-residency programs is available in Appendix D. Some of the more distinguished low-residency programs include Antioch University, Bennington College, Lesley University, New Orleans University, Vermont College, and Warren Wilson College.

A NOTE TO PROGRAM DIRECTORS

Johanna Foster is a graduate student in the creative writing program at Trinity College in Dublin, Ireland.

Q: What were your experiences with program Web sites?
A: "Some Web sites indicate 'We're friendly. Here's the information. If you have questions, let us know.' Others seem to say 'It's really hard to get into our program. You probably won't make the cut.' And a lot of them seem to say 'We don't really care about you or about designing a helpful Web site.' . . . This was really frustrating, because if you called a program, often the person on the line would indicate, 'You should know more about our program before you call,' but then there's not helpful information on the Web site. Where am I supposed to get this information?"

I'm probably the only person on this planet to have visited and explored the Web sites of every M.F.A., M.A., and Ph.D. creative writing program in the country. That's around three hundred Web sites, and it was not the easiest of experiences. If I had to hand out grades, there would certainly be a few As and B+'s, but overall, I'd put the median grade at around a D+. My goal in this short chapter is to urge program directors to push their Web site grades up to the B range.

If you feel like your program was misrepresented or misinterpreted in the previous brief profiles or the Appendix D information, then you are welcome to lodge a complaint. My e-mail address is easily found on the Internet. You are also welcome to place some energies and resources into your program's Web site, as that is the primary means of relaying vital information to prospective students. A poorly designed Web site is often interpreted as evidence of a poorly designed creative writing program. A Web site need not be fancy or flashy, but information should be clearly stated and found. If you care for advice, your Web site should contain the following information in an easily navigated site:

Admissions—What materials, specifically and easily summarized, are required for admission to the program? What is the due date? How many students are accepted out of, approximately, how many applications? An application should be online or easily downloadable in PDF and Word format.

About the Program—How many current students are in the program? Offer a sample schedule for your one, two, or three-year program. How many classes are students expected to take during which years?

Coursework—First and foremost: How many credit hours are required for the degree, and what classes are offered? Secondly, if there is flexibility in taking courses outside of the department, this fact should be noted. Often students like to take courses that will teach them about their particular writing interests, and these could range from biology to photography to political science.

Funding—If you feel like you provide solid funding for your graduate students, then state the specifics. What percentage of students are funded fully and partially? Specifically, how many teaching and other fellowships are available?

Location—A few words about your city, town, or other locality is welcomed. Yes, this information is often available on the university's main Web site. So, why not at least copy this information onto the program's Web site or provide a link?

Faculty—Most sites are pretty good about this. A list of faculty and their experience and publications is appreciated. If they have creative work posted on the Internet, then I'd encourage you to link to it.

Alumni—If your past students have had some success in the publishing or academic world, do you know about it and, if so, why aren't you bragging about it? Prospective students are interested in this information. If you are interested in your alumni, then this is a good sign that you are interested in your current students.

History—Every program, even a beginning one, has a history. Students are interested in what they will be a part of. Don't be afraid to tell a story, even a brief one.

Opportunities—Is your program connected with a literary magazine or university press? State this, and provide a link. And, if there are opportunities for experience, paid or unpaid, for your graduate students, then state what those are. Some programs host summer conferences, readings in high schools, or other community outreaches. Make your prospective students aware of these events.

Readings—Yes, a list of past visiting writers is a good thing. A list of this year's writers is even better. How many visiting writers does your program host a year? Do you also host publishers, small or large, agents, and editors? Make this information available.

Current and Recent Students—It's nice to profile your faculty. It's even nicer to profile and celebrate your current students. A brief bio, and even a photo, of current graduate students goes a long way toward making them feel valued and appreciated. And it speaks volumes to prospective students.

Resources—This is an important aspect of program Web sites that, to my mind, is often lacking. What university resources are available in the areas of child care, diversity, housing, libraries, and even parking? A page of links in these areas and others is greatly appreciated.

Contact—The e-mail address of an individual who can answer questions is most welcome and appreciated.

Awards—Does your program offer any? If so, describe them and list past winners.

Program News—What's happening *now*? What is the latest information about opportunities, awards, publications, events, and changes in the program? This page need not be updated daily. Once a month is enough and appreciated.

Events—When and where will readings, colloquiums, and other events take place? This is as important to current students as it is to prospective students.

This advice might seem overwhelming, but that shouldn't at all be the case. The main criteria for a well-designed site is the actual information. Your department likely has a technology person on staff and, if not, your students are likely 'Net savvy. Why not offer one or two of them degree credit and/or a small stipend for posting and maintaining the site? Either way, it's important to involve students, as they will more clearly see what information is needed and how it should be presented in a clear way. Want a model? Check out the University of Indiana's Web site. The address is http://www.indiana.edu/~mfawrite/.

CHAPTER 4

The Application Process

> **George Saunders is a professor of creative writing at Syracuse University, where he was also an M.F.A. student in fiction. His works include** *Pastoralia* **and** *CivilWarLand in Bad Decline.*
>
> **Q:** How does the selection committee make its decisions?
> **A:** "Honestly, as a committee of three or four people we find we are choosing the same top fifteen applicants about 90 percent of the time. Our individual writing aesthetic doesn't seem to enter into it much, by which I mean 'realist,' or 'experimentalist,' etc. What we're looking for is some combination of intelligence and reader awareness. The writer knows the effect that he or she is shooting for, and they get it . . . As for choosing the final six students, it's a gut thing. We talk and think about who we would be excited to work with. If I find myself thinking, 'Well, I can't exactly think of a reason to reject this person,' then that basically constitutes a rejection. At our acceptance rate, I really have to feel, 'Wow, I want to talk with this person about their work. I'm excited about this work.'"

Most deadlines for applications to creative writing graduate programs fall between the beginning of December till the middle of February. The vast majority land in January. Make sure you know the deadlines for your schools, and stick to them. If you want to pay

FedEx a lot of money for overnight shipping, by all means wait till the last minute. Otherwise, be sure to send your applications a week in advance. Do note that there is no real advantage to sending your applications in extremely early, though there is no drawback, either.

As I've said before, an application for graduate programs will contain some of a combination of . . .

- The writing sample. About 25–30 pages of prose or around 10–15 pages of poetry.
- Three letters of recommendation.
- A personal statement.
- Undergraduate and continuing studies transcripts.
- GRE scores.
- The actual application form itself.
- An application fee. ($40–65 dollars)

And for Ph.D. programs, many M.A. programs, and some M.F.A. programs:

- A critical essay.
- GRE Literature subject scores.

One of the first things you'll want to do is make a chart, listing what materials are due to which schools. If you have an incredibly organized mind, then you can skip this step. For the rest of us, see the sample chart on the following page.

As I've also said before, I am highly recommending that you apply to eight to twelve graduate programs. Why? Because programs receive around one hundred to four hundred applications each year, and they accept around 5 percent to 15 percent of those applications. Don't let that discourage you. Believe in your writing. But spread your net wide, and keep your options open.

I recommend that you start your application process about two months in advance. Though, that's assuming that you've been working on your writing sample long before you even knew it might *turn into* a writing sample. Two months is especially relevant when asking for letters of recommendation. And for studying for and completing the GRE. If you've got less than two months, you're not sunk yet, but it's time to get in gear.

Materials	School One	School Two	School Three	School Four
Deadline	December 15th	January 10th	January 15th	February 1st
Writing Sample	yes	yes	yes	yes
Letters of Recommen-dation	three	three	two	three
Personal Statement	yes	yes, along with teaching philosophy statement	yes	yes
GRE Scores	no	yes	yes	yes
Undergraduate (and other) Transcripts	yes, to be sent directly to the program office	yes, include in application packet	yes, either	yes, either
Application	yes	yes	yes, plus two copies	yes
Fee	$45	$50	$40	$55
Other	reading list	none	critical essay	none

In chapter 4, I'll include a checklist of activities you'll need to complete. For now, let's dive into the Q&A about the materials in the application.

In actual work hours, how long will the application process take?

If you apply to eight to twelve schools, and not counting the writing sample or studying for the GRE, I'd say about thirty to forty hours. If you have the luxury, spread this time out. Work for a few hours, say, each Tuesday and Thursday night, plus Saturday mornings. Don't burn yourself out.

Keep in mind that the first application is the hardest. After that, you are re-using many of the same materials. The process becomes easier for each additional application.

How important is the writing sample?

There are many parts of this book that will cause disagreement (and I hope discussion) between writers, program directors, and professors. But one aspect that all interested parties will agree on: The writing sample is the most important element of your application. How important? It's the first thing committee members read, and if it doesn't measure up to their standards, your letters of recommendation, personal statement, transcripts, and GRE scores are completely irrelevant. If a committee receives three hundred applications from which they will choose eighteen students, then your writing sample will get you from the three hundred level to the final thirty level. And it can quite possibly make you a lock for acceptance.

The writing sample is weighted around 90 percent of total importance to the application. Is it intimidating, trying to get from the three hundred applicants to the final eighteen? Sure it is. But that's why you're spreading your net wide, applying to eight to twelve schools. And also, you believe in your work. It's quality work, and you need to put it out there.

Programs will want 20 to 30 pages of fiction or nonfiction, or about 15 pages of poetry.

Geoffrey Wolff is the director of the graduate fiction program at the University of California Irvine. His works include *The Art of Burning Bridges*, *The Duke of Deception*, and *The Age of Consent*.

Q: What is the committee's process for considering the applications?

A: "Our deadline is January 15th, and we have to make our selections by the second week in March. Michelle Latiolais and I read all the applications. We go first to the fiction submissions. If one story seems uninteresting, we try the other story. If there's nothing there, if it's flat on the page, no music, no surprises, we don't go any farther. All the rest—gorgeous transcripts, endorsements, heart-stirring ambition—won't matter at that point. What we're looking for is difficult to articulate but not to recognize. Conventional writing about conventional wisdom is not going to claim any choosy reader's attention."

Should I anticipate what kind of "aesthetic" each program prefers?

Others will disagree with this, but my answer is a definite no. Some programs may be known for postmodern work, others for "experimental," others for "traditional." Attempting to define these terms is asking for a big headache. You can't predict which professors will be the primary readers in a particular year of applications. Sometimes all the professors read the work; sometimes it's only one or two. Some programs use outside readers. Attempting to guess the preferred aesthetic of your readers is like attempting to guess what your opponent will do in a sporting event. It has its advantages, but in the end you should be concentrating on what you're going to do. Put your best work forward. At the end of the selection process, committee members are looking for quality first, aesthetic, a very distant second.

So, how do I choose my "best work"?

Your best work is likely writing that you have put a lot of time into, and it's work that has received feedback in a writing workshop or from other writers. It's polished work. It's writing that you have worked hard on, set aside, come back to, edited and expanded, deepened and clarified.

Keep in mind that you are not always the best judge of your own work. Before you send in your application, you should have two or three people read your writing sample "nominees." If you have twelve poems and need to choose eight, then give your work to people you trust, and get their opinion about which work is strongest. Same thing if you have four stories and need to choose two. Who should you ask? Writing teachers, definitely. Other writers that you know are another good source. But don't rule out non-writers who are good readers. People know quality work when they see it. At least most people do. Who do you know who is well-read? Who will give you an honest opinion? Your writing teacher from your undergraduate studies is an excellent candidate, but your roommate might very well be another. Your mom or dad might be of help to you in this case, but I'd doubt it. Let your mom or dad help you out in other areas of your life. I hope they think you're the greatest, but people who think you're the greatest and infallible are not likely to be the most honest readers. Siblings are closer to what you want, and friends and friends of friends who are readers and writers are closer still. Don't be afraid to ask. There's good karma in the world out there. Many people will be flattered that you ask. Get your work into other people's hands, and see what they have to say. You may be surprised in good ways and bad, but most certainly your assumptions will be both reinforced and challenged, and that's always a good thing for a writer.

At the end of the day (at the risk of my using two clichés in one sentence), go with your gut. Choose work that appeals to a broad audience and, at the same time, also go with the work that you truly believe in and that you've worked hardest on.

George Saunders

Q: How should students choose their writing samples?
A: "The bell curve holds true in my experience. You've got submarine detective stories on one end, beautiful work on the other. Everything else is in the middle. You've got to push your work to the beautiful end. What I mean is, you have to not do the things that anyone else can do. Go for the stuff only you can do."

We bet you have a personal story that will shed light on this particular aspect, huh?

Oh yes. For whatever it is worth.

When I applied to the Wallace Stegner Program at Stanford University (the Stegner Program is a two-year, non-degree fellowship program), I sent in two stories, "Groundskeeping" and "Bones." "Groundskeeping" was the old reliable: solid narration, description, and dialogue. "Bones" was something newer to me. It had a strong, unpredictable voice, and a changing, unpredictable narrative. "Bones" is three narratives in one, with no tangible connection between the three. My opinion at the time of my application? "Bones" was my kick-ass story, ready to change the face of the literary landscape. "Groundskeeping," on the other hand, was certainly solid, but nothing spectacular.

I also had a third story, similar to "Bones," and I thought very seriously of turning in the two newer works and leaving "Groundskeeping" out completely.

A year later, after being accepted, I was talking about "Bones" (the newer work) with one of the committee members who was a professor at Stanford, and whose identity will be protected. He/she said: "I liked 'Bones,' but it was pretty crazy. If you'd sent two 'Bones' in, you wouldn't have made the cut. It was 'Groundskeeping' that got you in." My point? If my friend Cathy Schlund-Vials hadn't said "You should definitely send 'Groundskeeping,'" and if I hadn't said, "Really?" and if she hadn't said, "Yes, dummy," then I wouldn't have been accepted. Get your work into the hands of your readers. Listen to what they have to say. It might be a good rule of thumb to send half the work that readers admire, and half the work (half the writing sample) that you feel strongly about. Hopefully, there will be overlap between these two opinions.

I followed other people's opinions and I also followed my gut, and that balance is what you should seek when selecting your writing samples. You can't predict what one committee will like and what another committee will not like. Send your best work, and a balance of it, and let the chips fall where they may.

Bruce Snider

Q: Any tips for the writing sample?
A: "Begin strong and end strong, but particularly begin strong. Put your best work at the front of your manuscript. Readers are often more likely to forgive things later if you prove that you know what you're doing from the outset. If you're going to take some risks, and you should, do so once you've established yourself."

So, I shouldn't send new work? Or should I?

If new work means work that you wrote a week or two before the deadline, then no, you shouldn't send that in. Allowing work to sit for a while is always a good idea. Its strength and its weaknesses will become clearer in time, and then those weaknesses can be fixed and the strengths can be expanded. Definitely send work from the last year or two of your writing experience, but don't send writing that is not yet fully formed.

Aimee Bender is a professor of English at the University of Southern California. She received the M.F.A. in fiction from the University of California Irvine. Her works include *The Girl in the Flammable Skirt* **and** *An Invisible Sign of My Own.*

Q: What advice would you offer for the writing sample?
A: "You could turn in the story you wrote years before that you received praise for, but it's wise to turn in work that you feel most connected to *right now*. You want to show the committee the direction you're interested in. You want to show them where you're going. You'll attract the same kind of teacher that way."

Should I send the same work to each school?

Definitely yes. Be consistent in what you choose and send. If you have stories, nonfiction, or poems A, B, C, and D, and your readers unanimously choose C and are split on A, B, and D, then definitely send C. If B is your favorite work, then send that with C, and send those two to all of your schools. Don't mix and match, hoping to get the right combination at the right school. Why not? Because if you don't get into any schools, then you'll know that B and C are not the works to send next year. And you should be reapplying the next year if you don't get in the first time around. You want to study writing, so don't be discouraged if you aren't as successful as you'd like the first time around. Learn from the experience, and change your strategy accordingly. And whether you do get in or not, you'll have been consistent with your choices, and you won't spend the next three months (as the applications are read and as you wait to hear either way) second-guessing yourself.

If the writing sample counts 90 percent, then what is the next most important element?

The next most important element is your personal statement, followed by the letters of recommendation. I'm actually going to start talking about the letters of recommendation first, though, since you'll need to ask for these early.

Keep in mind that the writing sample will get you into the semi-finals (say, into the top 30, from which 18 will be chosen). These next two elements will help or hinder you into the final group.

Hold on. What about the critical essay?

Good question. Again, the critical essay is likely a requirement for Ph.D. and M.A. programs only. My best advice is to use your best essay sample from your undergraduate or continuing studies English work. Read it again. Edit it. Deepen it. Expand and clarify. Give it to your readers, two or more of them, and ask for feedback. Make this critical essay your very best. This element will factor in heavily for prospective Ph.D. and M.A. students, right after the creative writing sample.

Who should I choose to write my letters of recommendation? What should I ask them to say? How should I go about asking them? Should I ask famous authors? What if I don't know anyone?

Whoa. All right, first things first. Keep in mind that committees expect these letters to *actually recommend* you, and to recommend you strongly. You want the letters to be good. A lukewarm recommendation can really damage your entire application. So, choose the people you ask carefully. First and foremost, choose people you can count on.

So, let's say that Emily Dickinson is still alive. If so, she'd be at least 175 years old. Let's say that you know Emily Dickinson in some capacity (or another famous living writer instead). Would a recommendation from Ms. Dickinson help your application? Yes. Definitely. If it's a strong recommendation. A genuine endorsement from a famous and well-respected writer will definitely catch the eye of the committee.

(Yes, I know she was not famous when she was alive, smarty-pants. Let's not confuse the issue here.)

But which letter is better? An average letter from Emily Dickinson in which she basically says that she liked that one poem she saw of yours and that you seem like a nice person, or the letter from the community college writing instructor who has seen you in workshop and revision, and who can highly recommend your work ethic, your benefits to a workshop, and your writing talent? That isn't even a competition. It's community college instructor hands down.

Keep that in mind as you consider whom to ask. Choose people who have insight into your ability as a student, and who will definitely recommend you. Remember that you will not see these letters, so you need to ask people you trust.

Peter Turchi directs the M.F.A. program for writers at Warren Wilson College. His works include *Maps of the Imagination: The Writer as Cartographer*, *The Girls Next Door*, and *Magician*.

Q: What advice would you offer about letters of recommendation?
A: "Letters of recommendation can be helpful if it's evident that the recommender has some insight into the applicant's work as a student and as a writer. Letters of recommendation from friends, colleagues, agents, editors, and acquaintances are not influential. Having a 'big name' recommender is not influential . . . Applicants should choose recommenders who know them as students and/or as writers, and they should choose them carefully enough that they can allow the recommendations to be confidential. The most influential recommendations are candid: they describe the student's weaknesses as well as his or her strengths. The same is true for whatever letter of application or personal essay the student writes: one of the most helpful things for application readers to see is how the applicant perceives his or her own strengths and weaknesses. Thoughtful self-analysis is more important than a witty phrase or even publication."

Okay, who will I ask then?

Any writing instructors from your classes are a definite on your list. But do consider other instructors you've had, in literature courses or even not in literature courses. Remember that the graduate committee wants to know one primary thing in this letter: Is this candidate ready for graduate school and will he/she be an asset to our program? And also remember that almost all the members of the committee are teachers. Who speaks the language of teachers best? Other teachers, of course. Choose people who can comment on your academic ability and promise.

Remember that the committee will have your writing sample in front of them. They don't need letters that go on and on about your writing ability. If they don't like your poems, then a letter saying how talented you are is not going to convince them otherwise. Your letters of recommendation are intended to fill in other areas that the committee might not be aware of: academic promise, ability to work within a writing community, your reliability, and your ability to get along well with others.

It's my opinion that at least two of your three letters should come from teachers who can comment on your effectiveness in the academic and writing world. The third could come from a teacher as well, but you can also look outside that world. Perhaps someone who has supervised you in a volunteer program. Or someone who has worked with you as you organized an event. It's important that at least one of these letters, preferably more, fills in the gap between your undergraduate years and today. This person might have an insight about you that the other letter writers are not aware of.

At the end of the day, go with someone you trust who can comment on your promise as a student. Go with what you've got. If you honestly don't know anyone, then it's time to start getting back into school in some way or getting involved in your local writing community.

We could really use a do's and don't list about letters of recommendation, preferably in bullet-point form.

The sense of entitlement in these questions is overwhelming. But, here goes:

- Do be polite about asking. No one owes you a letter.
- Do give your recommenders plenty of time to write the letters. Two months advance time, with all the supporting materials, is considered common courtesy. If you don't have two months, then get in touch with them immediately.
- Do send an addressed, stamped envelope to each recommender for each letter. If you're applying to ten schools, the recommenders will have to make nine copies of their letters. Make sure you send them ten envelopes, stamped, with the correct address on each letter.
- Do listen to me when I tell you to send stamped envelopes. Nobody likes the jerk who makes his recommenders pay for

postage. They are doing you a big favor. Make the process as easy as possible for them.

- Do ask them to write their letters on their organization's letterhead if possible.
- Do send a copy of your résumé to them. They may want to comment on aspects of your experience that they need to be reminded about.
- Do send the recommendation form that the graduate program provides.
- Do ask people who you can count on, and who will actually remember to write the letters.
- Don't send these things as you get them. Send each of your recommenders *all* of the material at once for *all* of the schools.
- Don't be afraid to ask your recommenders to comment on specific things, such as your work with revision, your participation in discussions, or your leadership abilities. Writing a recommendation can be difficult work, and if you offer your recommenders some suggestions, they'll be grateful.
- Don't hesitate to send a friendly reminder as the deadline nears.
- Don't forget to send a thank-you note after they've sent the letter. Your mother will be proud, and you may need a recommendation for something else in the future. No one likes a thankless task. Make sure that writing letters on your behalf is not one of those.

Before we get into your *long* advice on personal statements, is there anything you'd like to clarify in advance?

Yes. Most programs will simply ask for a personal statement or statement of purpose without much direction on how to complete it. That's why I'm offering my opinion below. On the other hand, some programs will ask for specific information to be addressed. Be sure to follow the guidelines and address their questions directly.

Okay, then, what can you tell us about the personal statement in general?

I guess the first thing I'd recommend about the personal statement is that you start early. Do write out a pre-draft of this about a month before the deadlines.

Do keep in mind that the personal statement should address your seriousness as a writer, some idea of what you'll do with your time in the graduate program, your experience related to writing, some of your interests outside of writing, a short bio, and some reasons (if possible) why you wish to attend this particular school. As with the letters of recommendation, I don't feel like it's very important, or even helpful, to address your writing head-on. Your process of writing—how long you've been working as a writer, how often you write, where you hope to go with it—is definitely important. But including a line like "My poetry's quality and style has often been compared to the work of Sylvia Plath" is not going to be very helpful at all.

I also don't think it's helpful to discuss your take on the state of twenty-first-century writing, or to include a list of writers you admire. Perhaps your favorite poet is Mary Oliver. In my opinion, she's a great favorite to have. But a member of the committee might not think so. Try not to tip your hand here. Certain applications will include a section for your favorite authors. Definitely state them there. But the personal letter should stick to the issue at hand: where you are as a person and writer right now (and where you have been), and where you'd like to go as a person and writer by attending this program.

If we've done some interesting things in life, like backpacking in Asia, or being the legal guardian of your little sister, or working as a UPS driver, or volunteering in the Peace Corps or Teach for America, or working as a hang-gliding instructor, should we include these in our personal statement?

Yes. Programs are definitely looking for well-rounded people, or at least rounding-in-progress people. I'd traveled in Ireland extensively, where my mother was born, and I wrote a few sentences about that in my statement. I'd also started and edited a literary magazine in North Carolina, and I wrote briefly about that. As a teenager, I'd worked on the NyQuil line at the Vick's (VapoRub) factory. No joke. I included a sentence about that. Writers use their experience in their writing. If you have some, let the committee members know about it.

These aspects should be addressed in only a paragraph or two in the middle of the letter. Talk about where you have been, where you are, but also be sure to have goals, and speak to them, about where you are going.

How long should the letter be?

The final letter should be between one and a half pages and two pages. No more.

How about some tips on the letter itself?

Look, before you sit down to write your letter, I think it's helpful to take stock of where you are in your writing and in your life. Though you may not use most of this information in your letter, it will be helpful in seeing yourself and your work in a clearer way. Sit down for forty minutes at your computer or notepad. Don't worry about what someone will think when they read this exercise. They're not going to. This is just for you. In fact, it may help if you write it in a "Dear Diary" format. So, relax and answer these questions:

1. What is the reward for writing? Why do you do it?
2. What three books have affected you the most in your life? Why, for each one.
3. What is your writing schedule (how often and where do you write)? And what would you *like* your writing schedule to be?
4. Describe the book you would like to write. Describe it on your own terms.
5. Describe your weaknesses as a writer. Describe your strengths.
6. What life events have affected your writing? What interesting things have you done (on your terms) that impact your writing?
7. What have you learned in writing classes, or other classes, that have impacted your writing?
8. How would an outside observer describe your writing?
9. When did you first start to write, and why?
10. Finally, why are you applying to these programs at this point in your life? What are you hoping to gain from this experience?

Wait a minute. Those questions address some aspect you told us *not* to address in our letter.

I know. This is not your letter. You're simply taking stock of where you are right now.

Would now be a good time to stop asking questions and to start writing?

Yes.

All right, we've written it now. It was easier than we thought, once we got going on it. Some things we wrote surprised us, in good and bad ways. What should we do now?

Set it aside for a day or two. Come back to it and reread. Think about it. Then put it away and don't look at it anymore. If you actually addressed those questions, then you know yourself better as a writer now. And that will help you write a better letter. If you didn't write this exercise, well, phooey on you.

Okay, tips on the personal letter now?

Yes.

- If you do nothing else, come across as a nice person. And a humble and curious person at that. Be someone who others want to work with.
- The purpose of the letter is to express your writing and life background, your goals for your time in the program, and your motivation for and dedication to learning.
- Organize the document in a formal letter form. Your name and address at the top (to the right of center). The date (below, to the right of center) The name of the program and its street address (on the left). And below (and on the left) you can simply address the letter to "Selection Committee."
- Don't be afraid to state the obvious: that you're applying to this program in creative writing and you're going to explain a little about yourself and what you'd do with your time in this program.
- Introduce yourself briefly. Name, age, writing experience, academic experience, where you've lived, what you've done.
- What are you currently working on, writing wise? Don't explain it, but briefly summarize it. Summarize any relevant work you've done in the writing world (editing, workshops, publishing, etc.).
- Note: You may reference, briefly, your writing sample, but don't end up explaining it. It has to stand on its own.
- Explain what you hope to gain by attending this particular program. What will you do with the writing time? What work do you hope to complete? What classes are you interested in? Explain that you enjoy the workshop experience and have benefited from it previously. Explain that you take your responsibilities as a student seriously. Same thing for literature

classes and your other experience. Explain why you value a community of writers. (I'm assuming all these things are true.) If you're interested in teaching, explain why and what you hope to contribute and receive from the experience. Same thing about literary journals if applicable, or community outreach.

- Always come across as a serious writer. A serious writer reads a lot and writes a lot. A serious writer, though, is not a know-it-all.
- Explain what you'd like to do, career-wise, after your graduate experience. It's just fine, and even preferable, to have your options open. But give them some idea.
- Summarize the most important points. Thank them for their consideration. Tell them that you will make the most of this experience.
- And do all these things in your own voice. My sense is that the tone should be "formal and friendly."

What if our letter turns out to be a mess?

It's probably better than you think. And in any case, it's the only one you've got. Set it aside again for a few days. Come back to it and edit it. Clarify and deepen. Make it consistent. Then, show it to two readers. Listen to their feedback and then again set it aside for a few days.

Finally, and this is very important: Do not edit the letter draft in the *original* computer document. Print out what you have, along with your notes for changes, and then retype the letter in a *new* document in your computer. This will help you keep the voice consistent and your points clearer.

Can we deviate from what you've recommended?

You do whatever you want. This is your letter. I feel strongest about including the personal life information and coming across as a serious writer and a nice person.

Should we reference specific professors in the program? Should we say that we've read their books and admire their work?

I'd say no. Especially if you're only referencing one or two of the professors. What if the third one reads your letter? My sense is that this will risk more harm than good.

Michael Collier is professor and co-director of the creative writing program at the University of Maryland. His works include *The Neighbor*, *The Folded Heart*, and, as co-editor, *The New Bread Loaf Anthology of Contemporary American Poetry*.

Q: What are some problems that committee members see in personal letters, and what advice would you offer to correct these?
A: "Often applicants don't seem to know anything about the programs they are applying to. This is because they use a generic letter. It's important that the personal statement be tailored individually to each program. This way an applicant can demonstrate the particular reason he or she is applying to that program. The personal statement should also convey something of an applicant's character and temperament, and from this can be gleaned their seriousness of purpose and sophistication as a writer."

Can I use the same letter for each program?

Sort of. You can use the bulk of the letter for each of the programs, but make each of your letters each specific in some way.

But *be sure* to change program-specific elements. This can be everything from addressing your letter to the Minnesota program as "University of Minnesota," and not the leftover from your previous letter to "Brown University" (yes, it's happened), to removing sections about teaching or working on program literary journals where that is not relevant to that program.

Get it right for each letter.

Final thoughts on the personal statement?

I guess I think of it as important. This is the only chance you have to talk about *you*. If you don't have the time necessary to write, rewrite, set aside, have others read it, set aside again, etc., then keep Teddy Roosevelt's mantra in mind:

Do what you can, with what you have, where you are.

Thoughts on GRE scores?

The majority of creative writing programs will require GRE scores as part of your application. How much will they count in your selection? In most cases, hardly at all.

The GRE scores are used primarily by the graduate school, as opposed to the creative writing program, for admittance to the university. The creative writing program chooses its candidates, then sends their applications on to the graduate school (basically, a department in the university) for approval. Your GRE scores need to be somewhere in the neighborhood of the scores of other graduate students at that university.

That said, you do need to take the GRE, and you should take it seriously. The GRE is offered throughout the year in computer-based format. It's not wise for me to list the procedures here. They seem to change every year.

My sense is that you need to register a month and a half ahead of time in order to find a date and location and to receive the preparation software. To receive definitive answers to these questions, go to www.gre.org.

Study for the test. Use the software and the practice tests that the GRE provides. Buy one of those GRE help books if you like. Take the practice tests, figure out where your weaknesses are, then brush up in those areas. There are definitely examples of writers who were accepted to the creative writing program but who were rejected by the graduate school. Don't be one of those people.

Do keep in mind that some university-wide fellowships are granted on the merit of undergraduate transcripts and GRE scores, so if you're applying for one of those, then yes, you should work hard to score well.

We sense that you want to clarify.

I actually want to emphasize: For the majority of schools, you do need to take the General GRE test, you do need to take it on time (so consider signing up *now*), and you need to prepare for it and do your best. But don't expect the GRE scores to be a consideration of the creative writing committee. Just remember that you can't get into the graduate school without them.

What about GRE Subject Tests?

The Literature in English Subject Test is mainly for prospective Ph.D. and some M.A. students. Do check each program's requirements. The reading list for the subject test is extensive, so you'll likely need many months to prepare. Go to www.gre.org for sign-up and preparation information. I don't know of any M.F.A. programs that require the subject test.

The Literature Subject Test scores will count heavily for prospective Ph.D. and some M.A. students, right behind the two writing samples (creative and critical), especially for programs that lean heavily on the literature component.

What about transcripts?

Send off for your undergraduate transcripts early. Some graduate programs will want originals, not simply copies, so make sure you send off for enough of them. Allow a month's time at least to get this process handled. You can normally order transcripts through your undergraduate university's home page. Some writing programs will want them sent directly to their offices, but most will allow you to include them with your application packet.

How much will your transcript count in your application? Not as much as your letter and your recommendations, but it might count some. But why worry over it? There's not anything you can do about those grades now.

What about the application form itself?

Some programs offer online applications (where you'll actually complete the application online and *submit* it online), and some programs will simply provide an application to download and print out. Programs that do not have at least a downloadable application seem very much behind the technological curve to me. You'll have to e-mail for the application to be sent to you. Hopefully they will have e-mail.

You'll get the usual in the application: name, address, etc.; optional questions about your ethnicity; non-optional questions about your residency and citizenship; a list of colleges you've attended; etc.

The application is normally straightforward, though there may be *two* applications. One for the creative writing program and one for the graduate school. Program Web sites are normally clear about this. If there is any confusion, I'd encourage you to e-mail the program coordinator.

In a few cases, the program application might ask you to indicate your favorite authors or other writing-related information. In other cases, the application may include a long list of questions. Go ahead and fill out all the information. Be clear and straightforward.

You do need to be clear and complete in your application, as an incomplete application may very well be dropped from the applicant pool before anyone even sees your writing sample. In most cases, the application itself will not be heavily considered in the selection process. But, obviously, you won't be considered as a candidate without completing it in full.

Other items in the application?

The application fee. Don't forget that, by check or money order. By the way, most of these will range from $40 to 65 dollars. Anything more than that and I'd seriously reconsider the program. An application fee should cover the cost of processing and the committee work. It shouldn't be a profit-making venture for the program.

It's also a good idea to include a self-addressed, stamped postcard with your application, whether the program asks for one or not. When you include a postcard, the program will mail it back to you, and you'll know your application arrived in full.

Some programs may have a more complicated application, with shorter essays in a variety of areas. Other programs may ask for a teaching philosophy statement. I know of one program that asks for a self-critique of an applicant's writing. Obviously, if a program asks for something in addition to the items I've listed, be sure to send it.

What if I have something else that they haven't asked for? Can I send that?

Few programs ask for a résumé or a c.v. (curriculum vitae). I think it's okay to send one if you feel like it. However, it should not stand in replacement of your personal statement. If a program is not interested in the résumé, they'll just toss it and keep what they need. That said, a résumé in this case should last only two pages.

I'm not saying you should send a résumé. I'm saying I think it is okay if you can't control yourself.

I hope this is obvious: I would recommend against sending newspaper clippings about yourself or a homemade video or the like. You'll seem amateurish and immature, whether that's the case or not. Stick to the items you've been asked for, and address other items in your personal statement.

Final thoughts?

Remember that your writing sample is, by far, the most important element of your application. In that sense, this is a very different application than your undergraduate application or for other graduate degrees. By your senior year in high school, you knew what your grades were and you knew what your SAT scores were. Consequently, you had a general idea of which colleges you would get into, and which you would not. It's similar for, say, law school graduate students when they factor in their undergraduate transcripts and their LSAT scores.

But for the graduate degree in creative writing, it's the writing sample, and almost the writing sample only. Ninety percent of how you'll be judged will be based on your writing. This element makes the "prediction" process very difficult. You don't really know where you stand a good chance and where you don't. So, it behooves you to send them your work and find out. And it also behooves you to apply to a number of schools (8–12) and, finally, you are behooved to control what you can control—your application and its contents, your criteria for selecting schools—and to not worry too much about the rest.

Chapter Summary

1. Your application materials for most creative writing programs will include: your writing samples, three letters of recommendation, a personal statement, undergraduate (and other, if applicable) transcripts, GRE scores, the application form, and the application fee.

2. Applications to Ph.D. programs and some M.A. programs will require GRE Literature in English Subject Test scores and a critical essay.

3. Apply to eight to twelve programs. Keep your options open.

4. The writing sample is, by far, the most important element in your application. Be sure to give your work to readers and writers and listen to their comments about the strength of the work.

5. For your letters of recommendation, choose people you trust who can comment effectively on your academic achievements and potential.

6. The personal statement should address: who you are, what you have done in your life, why you're ready for graduate work, and

what you will do with your time in the program. I wouldn't spend too much time addressing your writing directly. Do address your writing-related *experience*, but know that your writing sample must speak for itself.

7. The GRE and college transcripts are necessary parts of the application process in most cases. They don't count heavily, but you can't be accepted without them.

8. The application process can be complicated. Make a schedule and stick to it.

CHECKLIST FOR APPLYING TO CREATIVE WRITING PROGRAMS

_____ Read this book so you know what you're getting into.

_____ Decide on what criteria you'll use in selecting your programs. What tops your list? Funding, location, teaching experience, faculty? Make a list of must have's and a list of like-to-have's.

_____ Narrow your search to about thirty programs. They are listed by state at the back of this book, and there is also the profile of fifty in chapter three. Yes, by all means, include some of the "top" programs, but also include smaller, lesser-known programs. Spread your net wide and keep your chances for acceptance high.

_____ Read over the Web sites of these programs. Yes, all thirty of them. Break them into groups of five and read them over the course of one or two weeks. While you're moving along, keep a list of definitely apply, likely apply, and maybe apply.

_____ If you know people who have attended a creative writing graduate program, by all means do talk with them. They may have insights not only into their own program, but into other programs as well. And about programs in general. If it's a friend of a friend of a friend, don't hesitate to contact him or her. People enjoy talking about their experiences. You may pick up some tips or insights.

_____ If you are confused about anything involving a program, contact the program coordinators/administrators by e-mail. That's what they're there for. Do try and keep your questions limited to one e-mail. No one likes a noodge. And be sure to be polite. While program coordinators likely won't have a say in the acceptance process, they do work in the same offices as people who do. If you seem like a pain in the neck, then that word will get around.

_____ When you have the information you need, sit down and make your decisions about the twelve or so programs that you'll apply to. Include a mix of "top" programs and lesser-known programs. Be sure to talk this out with someone: a roommate, a sibling, a friend, even if the person has no experience in creative writing. Sometimes you simply need a sounding board to get your decisions organized. When you've made your final decision on the twelve, be at peace with them. You've done your research. You've used good criteria. Be happy about your choices, and don't second-guess yourself.

_____ Download or request materials from schools, including the forms for recommenders. Make an "organized" chart similar to the one at the beginning of chapter 4.

_____ Decide whom you'll need letters of recommendation from. Try to do this two months ahead of the deadline. Contact these people as soon as possible. You'll need three, so consider three and two backups. Contact the first three. Be clear about deadlines, and be sure, once they have said yes, to send them all of the materials they'll need in one package. Be polite and grateful. No one owes you a letter. Do send clear instructions with your packet. Some letters will go directly to programs; others will be sent to you in sealed envelopes. Include stamped, addressed envelopes in your packet for the convenience of the recommenders.

_____ Send off for transcripts from your undergraduate or continuing studies institutions. Allow two to three weeks for the transcripts to arrive. Be aware that most programs will ask you to simply include the transcripts with your application, though others will ask that the transcripts be sent directly to their office.

_____ Go to the GRE Web site. Sign up for the appropriate tests, either General or General and Literature. Give yourself a few weeks to study and prepare yourself. Give yourself more time if you're taking the GRE Literature in English Subject Test. Buy one of those GRE books or use the preparation material that the GRE provides, take the practice tests, and then work on areas necessary for improvement.

_____ Think about your writing sample. If you have four stories you're thinking about sending (you'll send only two), then give copies to readers you trust and who will give you an honest opinion. Give them to three or four people. Same thing if you have eighteen poems and will send only nine. Listen to what people have to say. Then, sleep on it for a week. At the end of the process, go with your gut. Send the work that you believe is the highest quality.

_____ Complete the writing exercise I've included in chapter 4. Think about where you are in your writing and in your life. This will be good preparation for your personal statement, and for your program experience.

_____ Take the GRE. My mom would say: Get a good night's sleep beforehand, and eat a good breakfast. That's good advice. Thanks, Mom. Have your scores sent to your schools.

_____ Be sure to polish your writing samples. Edit them and make them better. I don't recommend writing something brand new. By that, I mean an entire new story or poem. You may certainly add new sections to existing works. Go with your polished, complete work. Have someone read for copyediting and for consistency. Don't let a typo distract program readers from the quality of your work.

_____ Write your personal statement. Be sure to address the areas I mentioned in the previous chapter and, of course, the directions of the program. Be friendly and formal. Make sure you come across as a serious writer and a nice person. Set the statement aside for a day or two. Edit it. Give it to two readers. Listen to their comments. Make your final changes. Your final letter should be between a page and a half to two pages.

_____ Fill out copies of the applications in pencil. Figure out any problem areas you need to contend with.

_____ Fill out the applications in pen, or online.

_____ If you haven't heard back from your recommenders with two weeks to go before the deadlines, send a friendly reminder.

_____ Get everything together. Go back to your chart. Lay all the necessary materials out on the floor, in piles for each school. Double-check the contents. Then, send them off a week before the deadlines. Sooner if you want. If you're down to the wire, be aware that some schools require delivery by the deadline, and others require postmarks by the deadline. Use overnight delivery if you're pushing things.

_____ Take a deep breath. Go out to dinner with a friend. Celebrate a little. That was harder than you thought it'd be, but you got it done on time. Now, get back to your life, and allow your application to do its work. You'll hear back in early April, and there's nothing further for you to do till then.

_____ Nice job.

CHAPTER 5

Decision Time

Tracy K. Smith is a professor of English at the University of Pittsburgh. She received her M.F.A. from Columbia University and was later a Wallace Stegner Fellow at Stanford University. *The Body's Question* is her first book of poetry.

Q: How does one make a final decision about where to attend?

A: "I think one of the main things you can go on is a gut feeling, but only if you know what you're dealing with. Visit each of the programs. Sit in on a workshop. Get a sense of the workshop, and of the program. What will the community be like? Get a sense of the spirit governing the place. Students and faculty may change, but for the most part the environment will not. This will help you eliminate some programs from your list, and it will move you toward others."

Okay, you've sent your applications, you've returned to your normal life, and now you're waiting to hear. You'll start receiving responses in late March to early April. Decision time will come next. You'll likely need to choose from your options by mid- to late April and, in general, you'll only have about two weeks to make your decision. Make sure you're prepared for those weeks.

We've applied to eight to twelve programs. How many will we be accepted to?

You've applied to that many programs so you'd have some options. It would be best if you were accepted to three or more, but even two will offer some options for your final decision. You won't be accepted everywhere, simply because different schools and committee members have different tastes. For the purpose of most of this chapter, let's assume you've been accepted to three programs.

What if we're not accepted anywhere?

That's certainly a possibility. First of all, don't take it personally. You sent your work, you let the chips fall where they may, and they didn't happen to fall your way this time. I know of many current and former creative writing graduate students who were not accepted on their first try. So don't give up. Read a lot; write lot. Receive feedback on your writing. My best advice is: Shake your reading list up. Seek new work; read new work. Take a writing class. Apply again the next year, to a mix of schools: half where you've previously applied, half new schools. Send new work. Rejection is part of being a writer; so is perseverance. If you're serious about writing, then you can make this happen. Keep your chin up, and apply again in the fall.

You said that the criteria for our final decision will be different from the "preliminary" criteria. What should we be looking at now?

Funding moves up to a definite number one. If one program offers funding far and above your other acceptances, then I'd go with that one. A program that funds its students will support its students in other ways as well. If funding is similar, or if tuition is about the same, then move on to the other criteria.

Keep in mind that health care is part of funding, and we all know that health care is expensive. Make sure you know what kind of health plans are offered by the university, and factor this into your funding decision.

Location moves down to number two. You've already narrowed your original search to places where you want to live and places where you can stand to live. Now, if you've always wanted to live in New York City, or in rural Indiana, or on the coast of Florida, or the deserts of Arizona, go for it. Making a life for yourself in your new home is every bit as important as what you'll learn inside the program.

Teaching stays at number three, at least for most people. Most people will want teaching experience, but not *too much* teaching experience. Any program that makes you teach more than one class a semester is a program I'd be wary of. A program that offers teaching experience some semesters and writing or research or editing fellowships for some other semesters is a good choice. You'll want experience, and you may also want a break from that experience. I taught every semester when I was at UMass, and I actually liked that and benefited from it. So, one class a semester is about right. Above that is problematic, below that (but not none, obviously, if you want the experience) is better. Take stock of what classes you'll be teaching. You won't want to teach composition for three-years. Keep your eye on programs that offer experience teaching creative writing and other classes at some point during your career.

Faculty stays at number four, but there is more emphasis now. Read the work of professors in the program. You're not necessarily looking for similarities in your writing, though that may be a good thing. You're looking for writing that is interesting to you, and from which you might learn.

You left something out, didn't you?

It's not that I left something out, it's that I want to emphasize something in particular: Make sure, once you are accepted to a program, that you ask for contact numbers and e-mail addresses of current students. Call them up, talk with them, ask them about the program, campus, location, teaching experience, the general atmosphere, and especially the professors and other instructors. I'd recommend that you speak with at least three students at each school. Getting a "feel" for the program from its current students will guide you in great measure in your decision. Keep the main criteria in mind, but seek insight into the program from those who know best.

For the most part, current students are very happy to talk to newly admitted students. Make sure you have a list of a half-dozen questions before you call.

George Saunders

Q: What's the best way to research programs, especially the faculty?

A: "Always ask current students. I can't emphasizes that enough. One of the unknowns about faculty is, are they there? If William Shakespeare is on faculty, is he teaching most semesters, or does he teach one class every four years? It happens. Are they there for real, or are they just there on paper? Ask the current students. Students on the ground will know what it's like on the ground. E-mail is a great way to do this. A good program will facilitate you in contacting current students . . . Ask about the program director. The atmosphere of the program comes from the top down. If someone runs the program like a fiefdom, then that's something you want to stay away from. It happens. On the other hand, if someone shows affection for students, is interested in their work and in their lives, works to make them feel important and valued, actively promotes the community, then that's what you want."

Did you ask your interviewees for questions we should ask current students?

Of course I did. I'm always thinking.

Thanks to Rachel Kadish, Padma Viswanathan, Maria Hummel, Scott McCabe, and Aimee Bender for this list.

Obviously, you'll pick and choose as you see fit. Be a good interviewer, not an inquisitor, and you'll get the best answers.

- Regarding the city or town: Is the money you are given sufficient to live on? Is it isolated or urban? Is it safe or dangerous? Is the university integrated into the rest of the community? What are the rents in places where students live?
- How expensive is it to live? How do students make it?
- Are the program director and faculty responsive to student concerns? How much time and attention do you get from the faculty? What do you think of the professors as teachers of writing (as opposed to what you think of them as writers)?

- "I'd ask them how their writing is going. If I talk with three students, and they're all having trouble writing, then that's probably not a program I want to attend. That sounds obvious, but it's important."
- Does the workshop have a preferable style, and if you don't write that way, are you out of luck? Can different styles coexist in workshop?
- How much of a say do students have in planning their own curriculum? To what degree is the student an active agent in his or her personal and creative direction?
- "I'd want a general sense of the workload. A specific sense is even better. What is the workload? What is your life like as a student?"
- Do you think the progress you've made warrants your enrolling in the program? Have you seen substantial progress in your work that could not have been made on your own?
- What is the community within the program like?
- What do other graduates go on to do? Do they settle in that area? Do they publish? Do they get fellowships elsewhere? Do you receive some kind of counsel about how to move into the writing world after the program?
- What do you wish you'd known going in? What surprised you about the program?
- "I'd ask how has their writing changed. I want to know if the program encourages students to pay attention to that."

What if we're accepted to a program or programs, but we're not offered any funding?

Then that's a decision you'll have to make. You'll want to see if the tuition and other expenses are affordable for your situation. I would encourage you to talk to the administrator or, better yet, the program director at each of the schools. Tell him or her about your financial situation. There may be other funding options, or there may be a wait list for funding (in case other students do not accept offers, which is sometimes often). Keep your options open.

Some program directors may hold out hope of funding in the second year of the program. Take those comments with a grain of salt. In these cases, I'd bet your chances for future funding are about 50–50. If you're willing to take that risk, go for it.

And if you're not offered funding, but are determined to attend a program nonetheless, I'd encourage you to do so. Many programs, especially state universities, are affordable. Seek residency in the program's state, as this will reduce tuition greatly. Seek out jobs on campus, as these sometimes come with a tuition waiver. Apply for grants and fellowships that are offered by the university and by outside organizations. Work hard over the summer. Save your money.

I emphasize funding because I believe a writer should learn to live cheaply, at least early in his or her career, and because a program that funds its students is a program that supports its students. So, keep those things in mind. But also keep in mind: There are a number of hurdles to overcome in your writing career, and funding at your program may be one of those. If you're determined to improve your craft, to set aside time for your writing, and to become part of a writing community, then by all means make the financial investment in yourself. The one thing I would add is: Ask the program coordinator about current students who are paying full tuition. Get in touch with them by phone. Ask them about the program in general, but at some point ask about how the non-funded students are treated there. Many programs with fewer financial resources still offer other types of resources. If those current students are happy with their situation, then you likely will be too.

What if we're "wait-listed" for a program?

This is just what it sounds like. As an example, twelve students have been accepted for twelve slots at program C. But the program director knows that not all the students will accept the offer. So, there's a wait-list of a half-dozen students. If you're on it, feel free to ask what number you are. They may tell you; they may not.

If you're #1 on the wait-list, you'll likely be accepted, but I said "likely," not definitely. You should feel free to talk to the program coordinator or director about your chances. Don't be pushy, but ask directly and clearly. Make a good impression, as the phone call or e-mail might actually help your chances a lot.

Some schools don't have wait-lists at all. They'll look to gain twelve students by accepting eighteen. And yes, they'll take all eighteen if every student accepts, but that case is rare.

What if we have to make a decision at programs A and B, but we haven't yet heard from program C?

You should have heard something by April 15. Most programs will ask you to decide by mid- to late April. If program A is pressing you for an answer, don't hesitate to call program C and let them know that. Your tone should be, "I've been offered acceptance at one (or more) other programs, and I wanted to know when I might hear from your program. I've got to make a decision by the end of this week," and less of "What's the holdup? Don't you know I've got to make a very important decision here?"

By all means, get in contact. Phone is fine, e-mail is fine.

Remember that I said *If program A is pressing you.* Don't get on the phone with the other programs the minute you've been accepted to your first school. Keep a level head, and see what comes your way.

Can we "bargain" or "negotiate" with programs about funding?

To a certain extent. Do keep in mind: If a program funds all its students equally, or if there is no funding at all, then there is nothing to negotiate.

But let's say that program A offers great funding, but is located in a place you're not that excited about. And let's say that program B offers average funding, but is located in your favorite city and has an author on faculty that you're really excited about. There's nothing wrong with contacting program B and telling them the situation. They may very well up the ante. My funding was in doubt at UMass, and when I called to talk about it, I receive a "We'll see what we can do." As it turned out, they did a lot, and I had a teaching position two days later.

I doubt if a program director can give you an answer on the spot. But there's nothing wrong with making your needs and preferences clear and asking if there is some leeway with funding. Show your enthusiasm for that particular program and, again, see what comes your way.

Padma Viswanathan is a graduate student in the M.F.A. fiction program at the University of Arizona. She holds an M.A. degree in creative writing from Johns Hopkins University.

Q: Can students bargain with programs?
A: "I never thought of it as bargaining. I stated my needs and asked what options I had. At one time I had an offer from two schools. The first school's offer was not nearly as good as the second. I was very honest with them about it. They

came back to me with another offer which was much more substantial, though it still didn't quite match up. But then the second school increased their offer too, without my having said anything to them. I was just hesitating and thinking things over. I ended up taking the best offer . . . Almost all my correspondence was by e-mail. I chose this because I wanted to word it exactly. I didn't wish to alienate anyone. It's important to remember that all of these people are potential future colleagues. The advice I would offer students is to be honest and negotiate in good faith. You're not playing them off one another. You're simply seeking the best situation for yourself. Put it in writing so that you're saying exactly what you want. No more, no less . . . It was interesting that one program, that I did not attend, asked me to write a letter explaining that funding was a major factor in my decision. They wanted to use my decision in negotiations with the administration, to show they were losing students because of a lack of resources."

Should we really be contacting/calling/e-mailing the programs this much?

I never said to contact the programs/directors/coordinators/current students all the time. Don't become an annoyance. Get your questions in mind and make the most of each contact.

Will programs offer an Admit Weekend, where we can visit the program?

Not many will, but some do. I think very highly of these programs, and so should you. It shows that they are actively recruiting their graduate students, and that they have the resources and initiative to do so. Definitely attend the weekend, and see what you can find out.

Can we defer our acceptance for a year?

In some cases. I'd say about a third of schools will allow you to do this if you have a good reason. But if you don't have a good reason, why hesitate? Go.

Hey, this is a big decision here. This is our lives we're talking about here. Why is this the last question in this very short chapter?

You're right, this is a big decision, and I'm not about to make it for you. When you're accepted to a program, visit their Web site again. Refresh your memory about their strengths and weaknesses. Talk to the program coordinator and director. Definitely, definitely, definitely talk with current and former students. Ask questions about whatever is most important to you: classes, program atmosphere, the feel of the town or city, health care, readings, publications, and other opportunities.

If you have the resources to visit your accepted programs, do so. Check it out firsthand.

Make a list of the pros and cons of each program. Sit down and talk them out with someone. A good friend, writer or not. Someone who is a good listener and who will tell you what he or she "hears" from you. Explain your criteria and how each program measures up or not. Talk about what you want to experience in the next two or more years, and how each program might fulfill your needs. Don't allow the person to make the decision for you, but instead ask him or her to repeat back what he or she hears from you. His or her best role is to help you organize your thoughts and to reflect back your own opinions.

Lean towards funding heavily, but keep your other criteria in mind. Make your decision. Sleep on it. If you feel good about it in the morning, you'll feel good about it for the years to come.

Congratulation on your acceptance(s). Make your decision. And make it your own.

Chapter Summary

1. Acceptances and rejections will start arriving in late March and early April. You'll need to make a final decision on your program by mid- to late April.

2. Criteria to use in your final decision: Funding is a definite one, and health care is part of funding. Location stays at number two. Teaching experience is three, whether you want teaching experience or you *don't* want teaching experience. Either way, stay away from programs that offer *too much* teaching (more than one

class a semester). Faculty stays at four, but is more important for this final decision. Read the work of your potential professors and see what you think.

3. The most important action you can take is to talk with current and former students about their experience in the program. Talk with at least three students from each program to get an accurate read on the atmosphere and resources of the program.

4. If you are not accepted to any programs, don't take it personally. Many current and past creative writing graduate students were not accepted on their first application. Read a lot, write a lot over the next few months. Shake up your reading list. Create new work, and apply again. Include new schools in the fall.

5. If funding is not offered at any of your accepted programs, then talk to the program directors there about other sources of financial support. Talk with current students about how less-funded students are treated in the program. Make your decision based on these conversations and of course your current financial situation.

6. Do contact programs if you haven't heard from them by April 15. Be clear about when you have to make your decisions about other programs. Do this also for any wait-listed schools. Be polite.

7. I'm not sure if "bargain" is the right word, but you can make your offers from programs clear to the directors of other programs. Do ask if they can match that offer. There's no harm in asking, and sometimes there is great help in it.

8. Talk out the pros and cons of each program with a friend. Ask that person to repeat back what he or she has heard. Use your criteria, and lean heavily on funding. Make your decision, sleep on it, and see if you feel right about it in the morning. Make your decision your own.

CHAPTER 6

Your Graduate Program

Geoffrey Wolff

Q: Do you have any advice for students entering a program?
A: "Students are naturally shocked at the amount of work they enlisted for. They take a course about teaching, they teach, they prepare work for workshop, they study and comment on their colleagues' work. Then they endure what Camus termed the fleas of life: where to live, how to furnish it, where a car can be repaired, who's a good dentist, where do you go to have a good time? It can be overwhelming. That's why it's crucial to stay awake during the summer before the program starts. Write up a storm that summer. Arrive with new work. That's the most profitable advice I can offer: Hit the ground running, and you'll be happy."

All right, you've arrived. Or are about to. Having a plan or at least some goals when you arrive is a key. What are those goals and plans? That's not really any of my business. My goals when I arrived at the University of Massachusetts were to complete a book, improve my writing, make some friends, learn to teach, live a variety of experiences, keep my sanity and health, and keep in touch with my friends and family. For the most part, I accomplished all of these things.

Read this chapter over. I hope to provide some insights about what you can expect in your program. Afterwards, take a few minutes and write down some goals for yourself, as well as some plans for getting these accomplished. By all means, stay loose, stay flexible, but keep one eye on the goals you've set out for yourself.

If you only had one piece of advice about our program experience, what would that be?

That's easy: You'll get out of it what you put into it. Be sure to enjoy your experience, but remember that part of that experience (and enjoyment) is rolling up your sleeves and getting to work. Furthermore, don't expect someone else (faculty, other students) to make a plan for you. Be your own advocate, and seek out the resources and experiences—classes, attention from instructors, outside writing groups, editorial or teaching experience, any variety of things—that you need and value.

Should we visit the program and city/town before the program starts?

Definitely yes. I'd suggest traveling there a month ahead of time. Why? Because this will facilitate finding a necessity: housing. (More soon.) You'll also meet the program coordinator, perhaps a professor (keep in mind that they are often away for the summer), and get to know the campus. Take a campus tour. Get in contact with a few second- and third-year students. E-mail them directly once you get contact information from the coordinator. And when I say e-mail them directly, I don't mean sending out a mass e-mail. I mean writing three or four students directly to say hi and to ask if you can talk with them about the program over the summer. Then get back in contact with them before you arrive. See if you can meet up with them for coffee. Maybe they'll offer to show you around town or introduce you to other students.

If someone offers to put you up for a night, take him or her up on the offer. Otherwise, check into a local hotel. A three-or four-day stay sounds about right.

What about housing?

The program coordinator should have some advice on this. But the best advice will come from current students. Some former students may be leaving, and you might check out their former residences. Check the classifieds online before you go. Set up appointments with landlords. It is *very* important to get suggestions on parts of town, or towns outside of the town, from current students before you go.

Don't be afraid to ask. Many programs include a survival guide written by students, on their Web sites. Study this thoroughly.

My best advice? Visit five or six apartments. If at all possible, sign no more than a six-month lease, unless you're really in love with a place. Keep your options open. You may find another neighborhood or a roommate situation you like better.

Arrive with your checkbook, and the phone numbers and addresses of previous landlords. If you don't have these things, you're sunk. So be sure to pack them.

Will you live with roommates or get a place by yourself? Depending on your financial situation, and your relationship situation, and the cost of living in that area, this question may have one or more answers. Do think about it ahead of time. Explore both options if you're not sure. Explore the option of living with current students, but definitely explore the option of roommates outside of the program. Having a life outside the program—especially after the first half year—can be important to your sanity.

I guess my best advice is to visit the location, tour around, visit as many rooms/apartments as you can, then sign a short-term lease.

If it's not possible for you to visit ahead of time, then do what you can in the first few days you arrive, using this same advice.

If I'm moving to another state, should I become a resident?

Definitely yes. As soon as possible. On a very basic level, you'll be aided by having in-state tuition, which will be helpful if you're paying for your education, or if your funding level is subject to change. On a more complex level, your residency will aid you in aspects from driver's license, voting, and eligibility for everything from library cards to grants and fellowships.

Go to the new state's main Web site and find the information about becoming a resident. Some states will make this easy; others, difficult. Either way, get it done.

What sort of class load should I take?

I'd recommend taking a high number of classes right from the beginning. By high I mean three or four. Why? First, it will immerse you in the program. You'll meet many more of your fellow students that way, as well as many of the professors. Second, you'll either be ahead or you'll be on schedule to finish your classes by the end of your stay. You'll appreciate extra time later, especially as you begin to think and work on your thesis.

Which classes should I take?

A workshop will likely be required each semester of the first year. There may be some specific required first-year classes. Obviously, take those. Otherwise, a contemporary fiction, poetry, or nonfiction class is always a good bet. Go ahead and concentrate on the required courses for your first semester and year. Save your electives and other flexible classes for when you're clearer about your interests and needs.

As always, ask veteran students about the best teachers and classes.

Maria Hummel

Q: Any classes that were particularly helpful to you?
A: "One class that was very practical was Editing and Publishing. I learned all the typographical marks. We wrote papers about the publishing world. I did one paper on the gutting of the mid-list in children's fiction and one on poetry contests. The class made me consider the publishing world as an industry, and, depressing as it was, that helped me to be realistic and informed in my goals. Later, I also ended up working as an editor to support myself, so the course was very useful to me."

What can you tell us about teaching, and about workshop?

I've included longer sections on these in chapter 6.

What about the social aspect of a graduate program?

What to say, what to say . . . First off, you'll likely notice that there are stark similarities between the first year of graduate school and the first year of undergraduate school. By that I mean, you're suddenly placed in a new situation, meeting lots of people, learning new ideas, reading new work, socializing in different places, and becoming a new person. To some extent or another. For lack of a better term, there's a kind of giddiness to the first year of graduate school. People stay out late, they make new friends, maybe an enemy or two, they gossip about others, they fail at things, succeed at others. By all means, enjoy all this. But keep grounded in some way. I think it's a very good idea to create an outlet *outside* of the graduate program. That may be a weekend job at a restaurant, a yoga or dance or drawing class, joining a gym, hanging out with non-writer neighbors, or joining a running or rock-climbing club. Whatever seems best to you. Keeping an aspect of your life outside of the program will pay huge dividends: You'll have a place to decompress from the pressures and thrills of graduate school, you'll be able to keep your graduate experience in perspective, and, therefore, you'll be able to enjoy it to a greater extent.

As far as the graduate program goes: there will be readings, seminars, on-campus events, and program parties. Informally, workshop members may meet at a bar or coffee shop after class, there will certainly be graduate student parties, some students may form reading or studying groups, and there will be weekend outings and road trips. Make friends, meet new people, make time for these events. Enjoy yourself. These may be some of the best years of your life. (Music swells, light dims, sun sets in the distance. . . .) But keep an outlet so you can keep it in perspective.

And don't forget the life you had before graduate school. Make time for family and friends, either by visits or by phone and e-mail. Do go home or travel during your winter and spring breaks and some longer weekends. Don't lose sight of where you've come from, even if you're headed somewhere else.

Maria Hummel

Q: Any advice on the social aspects of a program?

A: "Do get to know your classmates. Some of my favorite memories of the program were ad hoc dinners with my friends Michele, Jenn, and David. We'd pass around books. We'd say, "Have you read this? Isn't this great?" I learned as much from those nights as I did from workshop. It was an extension of the classroom, but with cheap red wine . . . We're sometimes isolated as writers, and when you get to an M.F.A. program it may be the first time in your life that you're surrounded by creative freaks like yourself. It's exhilarating. That said, don't let it take over. You have a lot of time, and that's good, but you can't party with your friends every moment. Most of us only get that two years. Make sure you're using that time for writing."

We've got a partner/girlfriend/boyfriend who we're going to do "long-distance" with. Any tips?

Well, my best advice is to go ahead and break up now, and save both of you a lot of trouble.

Funny, funny, ha, ha. But, I'm only being half funny. Or trying to be. You're going to immerse yourself in a lot of new experiences, and you're going to meet a lot of new people. Consequently, your long-distance relationship is going to feel a lot of strain. What I can tell you is this: When a partner/girlfriend/boyfriend moves with the graduate student, then all will likely be well. When the couple has a plan to be together within a year, all has a good chance to be well. When the couple has ambiguous plans to eventually be together at some unspecified time in the future, they're sunk.

So, if you value your relationship, either move together to the new town, or make plans to be together in the very near future (no longer than a year). Lack of a plan will likely result in lack of a relationship.

What's your best overall advice for making the most of our first year?

I've said this before, and I'll say it again in the teaching chapter: Make sure you speak with and learn from veteran students. Meet with them, buy them a cup of coffee, ask questions, listen. They have all sorts of insights that will help you avoid pitfalls and help you make the most of your graduate experience.

What about writing? Isn't that what we're here to do?

It sure is.

- Set aside a place for your writing. That may be a separate office in your apartment if you have room. It may be a desk moved into a corner. It may be a favorite table at a coffeehouse or library. Set aside a place where you will write, and write only. That place will be for your creative work, not for checking e-mail, surfing the Web, answering the phone, grading papers, reading for class, or any other distraction. Save a place for writing, and your writing will prosper.
- Set aside time for writing. Set a schedule, and stick to it. This may vary from writer to writer, but I'd suggest four or five blocks of time each week, two to four hours, where you will

work with your writing. Write out the schedule and post it somewhere. Keep it a priority.

- Write every day. Four hours would be great. But on your busier days, even simple outlines/notes/scenes/stanzas in your notebook for fifteen minutes can help a lot. Keep in practice with your writing, and it will take less time to get warmed up when you actually have large blocks of time in your writing schedule.

- Work on a few projects at once. I'm not talking a dozen. I'm talking three or four. They may be in different stages: first draft, editing, final draft, fun. When you get bored with one, or if you're blocked with another, you'll always have something to work on. Sometimes it helps one work when you ignore it consciously to work on another. Often, your unconscious mind is still working on the other.

- How can you deal with writer's block? Balance your time. You are outputting onto the page, so make sure you input in your life. Be *with* people. Get out and exercise. Do things at night or in the morning that are not writing related. Travel. Indulge another artistic expression such as drawing, photography, or music. Don't allow these to infringe on your writing schedule, but do schedule them, even for short amounts of time in the rest of your life schedule.

- The best cure for writer's block is reading. Read a lot, write a lot, and at appropriate times receive feedback on your writing. If you've been staring at the computer screen for too long, pick up a book and dive into it for a half hour. Often, seeing words on the page will jumpstart your own words. I think people often worry too much about being overly influenced by a work dissimilar to their own. Dissimilar work can actually be a big help. You can see what you want to do that is different, or you can learn techniques and craft that is applicable to your work. If you can't write, then read. And then write.

- Don't be discouraged by what you read. By that I mean: If you read your favorite writer and then despair about your own level of craft, that's not helping you. The solution is *not* to stop reading great work. The solution is to allow yourself a draft. Get words on paper, then see what to do about them. Do what you can with what you have, where you are. I'm not saying that you are a novice at the craft, but I am saying that all writers were novices at some point. We are all working to improve.

Allow yourself that goal of improvement. It comes in stages, not in leaps and bounds. Be steady and consistent, and you'll make your progress.

- If you're really stuck, then getting an outside opinion can be of great help. Give your work to a friend, or a fellow student, or a professor. Listen to what he or she has to say. You may simply need a nudge in a direction or two to jumpstart your creative mind.

What can you tell us about public readings?

Go to them. Especially when your fellow students are giving them and when the program has brought in an outside writer. Or, obviously, when one of your professors is reading. You'll support your colleagues and program. And you'll likely hear great or at least interesting work, and you'll have the chance to socialize afterwards.

How should we interact with our professors?

Get to know them. This can be informally, after class or after readings, or formally, during class or in office hours. The vast majority of creative writing professors care about their students and their students' careers. Read the work of your professors, and be familiar with it. Ask for advice about your creative work, your career options, a reading list. Speak to veteran students about which professors are helpful and insightful.

Victoria Chang holds an M.F.A. from Warren Wilson College, and she is currently a Ph.D. candidate at the University of Southern California. Her first book of poetry is *Circle*.

Q: What's the workload for a low-residency program?
A: "They'll tell you that it's 20 to 25 hours a week, and that's pretty accurate. It's good practice for living the life of a writer. It teaches you good habits. I spend 20 to 25 hours a week on my writing now, and that's because of the program. You get what you put into it. It's difficult, but you get used to it, and if you're serious about it, you look forward to that time."

It seems like a lot of these answers have to do with residency programs, as opposed to low-residency programs.

I think so too. That's why there's a great interview with Scott McCabe, a graduate of the Lesley University low-residency program later in this chapter. Check it out.

What can you tell us about publishing and literary magazines?

See the last section of this chapter "Publishing in Literary Magazines."

How do I get a literary agent?

I knew this was coming. First of all, this is likely for fiction and nonfiction writers primarily. Poets often enter their manuscripts in book contests, as do many short story writers. There are links to contest information in Appendix C.

In any case, here are my thoughts on agents. I emphasize the word *thoughts*:

Before you look for an agent, you should have built up a résumé of magazine publications. Somewhere around half a dozen sounds right. You'll likely be looking for an agent after your graduate experience, when you've completed a book to your satisfaction. Let me repeat that: You look for an agent when you've completed a book to your satisfaction. Your graduate experience is about learning your craft and concentrating in reading and writing.

Some people find agents through referrals. People who might refer you are friends, professors, or fellow students. Keep in mind: A referral is a big thing. No one is going to refer you to his or her agent if he or she is not enthusiastic about your work. Make certain that is the case before you ask. Otherwise, you're likely to be turned down, and you'll likely turn that person off.

The main thing you need to do is buy *Guide to Literary Agents* by Writers Digest Books. Read it thoroughly, especially the advice sections. Pay close attention to advice on query letters, as this is how you start the process of contacting an agent. There are listings of hundreds of agents and agencies in the book. Do think about the writers you admire who write in similar ways to you. Research their agents, in the book and on the Web.

How can you figure out which agents represent which writers? C'mon, this is the Google age. Get with it.

One of the most important aspects in finding and selecting an agent is the query letter. In the letter, list your experience and publications, state why you are interested in this particular agency, and explain in a couple of paragraphs about the work you are seeking to sell. Yes, you sometimes hear about writers who sell a novel or other book based on a first chapter or simply a proposal. But for the most part, publishers (and therefore agents) seek work from beginning writers that is complete or near-to-complete. Ask in your letter if the agent would be interested in seeing part or all of your novel or book.

Likely, you'll receive word back in two to three weeks. Send immediately to any agent who asks to see your work.

So, make sure you have a completed book when you query agents. And make sure it is polished and near to ready for publication.

As for choosing an agent and signing a contract, I'll not speak much to that. You want to find an agent with some sort of track record in closing deals. On the one hand, you want agents with a long list of clients and, on the other hand, you want an agent who will pay attention to you. If you are offered a contract, ask a professor about it. Or a published author whom you know personally. Again, *Guide to Literary Agents* has information about this.

At the end of the day, you want an agent who is clearly enthusiastic about your work, and who is likely to place it with a publisher. Pay attention to any contract offer you receive, and read the fine print.

I hope this goes without saying, but perhaps it doesn't: Any agent who asks for a "reading fee" or any sort of money from you is not an agent you should spend any time with. A serious agent believes in your work, and is confident in his/her success in placing it, and of course receiving his/her 15 percent of that deal. A serious agent also believes in your long-term success as a writer: not simply placing this one book, but also placing future books with publishers.

I want to reiterate: If you're just entering a program, don't worry about agents. This information is for your future use. Concentrate on your craft and your community.

Maria Hummel

Q: What about life after the graduate degree?
A: "Most people I've known have spent the two years—after their two years in an M.F.A. program—completing their

book. That's why funding is important when you choose a program. Consider an M.F.A. as the first or second step on the ladder, not the final rung. You won't want to come out heavily in debt with student loans. You'll want to keep writing, and that's harder when you have to work full time, or more, paying off loans. Even some of the best writers I know succeeded in publishing their first books long *after* their M.F.A. program, and it took some up to a decade to do it . . . The M.F.A. experience is rich and rewarding, and it also shakes you up a bit, and can confuse your perspective on your own work. Sometimes workshop can be *too much* response. It takes a while to let those workshop voices in your head settle down. When you begin to work in isolation again, with your own voice in your head, that's when you make your true progress."

How do we go about choosing our thesis committee?

A thesis committee is normally three professors who will read your final thesis (a book-length manuscript of your creative work) and offer questions, comments, suggestions, and insights. Sometimes there is simply one thesis advisor and no committee. Either way, you'll choose your reader(s) near the beginning of your last year in the program. Your primary thesis advisor is, obviously, the most important member of your committee. Choose someone who understands your work, is both encouraging and critical, and who will make him- or herself available for a few meetings throughout your final year.

Members of your committee are likely to be the professors in your creative writing program, but in most cases you can also choose professors from the English department, an elective department, or other professors who will have insight into your work. Your main advisor will likely be one of the fiction/poetry/nonfiction professors. Department and program chairs are often very flexible about allowing you to choose whom you want.

What sort of careers do post-graduates go into?

The creative writing degree is an artistic endeavor primarily, and a professional degree second. Graduates move on to careers in a variety of fields, but they all keep (or should keep) writing a priority in their lives. Graduates teach on the university or high school level, they become editors and Web designers, they write in the business world, they become journalists, they work as administrators in education, and sometimes they go on to other degrees in law, political science, and education.

Don't expect your degree alone to open up limitless opportunities in the teaching and publishing world. That said, the degree *will* open up opportunities in your creative endeavors.

And by the way, I would strongly recommend that you work as an intern during one of your summers in the program. This might be at a publishing house, a newspaper, a literary journal or other magazine, or in an educational or business setting. Working as an intern can lead to later employment, either with that organization or with another. The Associated Writing Programs (AWP) has listings of positions, as does the magazine *Poets and Writers*. (See Appendix C for more information.) Searching the Web is a good way also, as is asking your program coordinator.

Toward the end of your first year, make an appointment with the head of the program to talk about what steps you should take to plan your professional life after graduate school.

Michael Collier

Q: What advice would you offer for post-graduates?
A: "You have to protect your identity as a writer all the time, because so many things in our culture work against being a writer. This is true for all writers, including those who have full-time work in a university. If you teach English at a high school, you have to think of yourself as a writer who happens to teach English at a high school, and not as a person who was once in a graduate program as a writer and who now teaches English in high school. It's an important distinction . . . If you write software during the day, you have to think of yourself as a writer of poetry or fiction or nonfiction, not just at night, but all the time. Keep involved in your community of writers. Keep in contact with your classmates. Keep writing. This sense you have of yourself as a writer should override everything else. If you can't convince yourself that you're a writer, then you're not going to get the work done."

Do you want to remind us of something?

Yes I do. It's something I wrote at the beginning of this chapter: "Read this chapter over. I hope to provide some insights about what you can expect in your program. Afterwards, take a few minutes and write down some goals for yourself, as well as some plans for getting these accomplished." Guess what? It's almost afterwards. What do you want to get accomplished over the next two or three-years? Get writing.

Agents, long-distance relationships, thesis committees, careers . . . our heads are spinning. Can you center us in some way?

Yes I can. It's called Chapter Summary.

But before we get to that, relax. You're about to have a great and memorable experience in your life. Over the next few years you'll concentrate on your writing, you'll grow as a person, you'll be part of a writing community, you'll have new experiences and meet a variety of people. Work hard. Push yourself. Have fun.

There are a few more stops on the tour, but that's about it for the bus driver. I hope our time together was helpful to you. I enjoyed the tour, as I hope you did. Get out there now and explore the city. Find what you need. Check out those side streets. Happy trails, and rock on.

Chapter Summary

1. Visit your new program before the school year begins in order to take care of housing and to meet fellow students and professors. Make residency status in your new state a priority.

2. Make sure you speak with and learn from veteran students. Meet with them, buy them a cup of coffee, ask questions, listen. They have all sorts of insights that will help you avoid pitfalls and help you make the most of your graduate experience. This is the most important advice in this chapter.

3. Take three or four classes each semester of your first year. This will help you get acclimated to the program, meet new people, and get some requirements out of the way.

4. Take part in the social aspects of your program, both formal and informal. Attend readings, seminars, parties, and other

get-togethers. Keep or create outlets for yourself outside of the program to keep things in perspective. Take a yoga or art or dance class. Join a gym. Take a part-time job. Make friends outside of the program. Keep in touch with old friends and, of course, your family.

5. If you value your current romantic relationship, either move together to the new town or make plans to be together in the very near future (no longer than a year). Lack of a plan will likely result in lack of a relationship.

6. Set aside a place and time for your writing. Make a writing schedule and stick to it. Write every day, for as much as five hours or as little as fifteen minutes. Don't be afraid to work on a few projects at once: This will keep your mind fresh and will prevent boredom with one single project. Seek new experiences so that you have new input for your writing. Remember that the best cure for writer's block is reading. Read a lot, then write a lot. Get feedback on your writing at appropriate times from collaborators and colleagues.

7. Get to know your professors, formally or informally. Read their work and be familiar with it. Ask for advice about your creative work and about reading lists.

8. Seek a literary agent once you have built up a body of small publications *and* when you have a larger work to sell. Seek the agents of writers you admire and who write in a similar way to you. Send query letters and use *Guide to Literary Agents* by Writer's Digest Books.

9. For your thesis committee, choose a primary advisor who is familiar with your work, who is encouraging and also critical. Think about who you'd like for your committee at the beginning of your final year.

10. Graduates of creative writing programs take jobs in a variety of fields. Teaching and editing, of course. But also Web design, journalism, administration, business, and, of course, many graduates go on to other advanced degrees. The creative writing degree is an artistic endeavor primarily, and a professional degree second.

That said, keep an eye on your post-graduate career, especially after your first year. Seek summer internships and talk with your program director about steps to take to create career options.

LOW-RESIDENCY PROGRAMS:
AN INTERVIEW WITH SCOTT MCCABE

My interview with Scott McCabe, a graduate of the Lesley University M.F.A. program, was particularly helpful in regard to understanding low-residency programs. I've decided to include the bulk of that interview here. Thanks, Scott.

Q: Can you talk about the structure of your low-residency program?
A: "Each semester begins with a ten-day intensive residency. We meet for workshops and seminars, and for evening readings. Then, at the end of the residency, we break our own ways and work one-on-one with a faculty mentor for six months or so. There aren't really classes in the traditional sense. It's hands-on, active learning; students get to help shape their syllabi and spend much of the time teaching themselves. At Lesley University there are three lines of work: creative writing, craft reflection and annotations, and interdisciplinary work. The interdisciplinary work is an opportunity to pursue a medium that helps inform our creative writing. Some people work in graphic design or illustration; others, playwriting. A friend worked as an intern for a small local publisher. I worked on the art of the author interview, learning another way to make a living as a working writer."

Q: What are the craft reflection and annotations?
A: "I'll work independently for a month, writing and reading. I'll read two to three books in that time. The annotations are focused on craft: this or that aspect of technique. We write two to three pages and, generally, the closer the focus the better. One month I read the collection *Werewolves in their Youth* by Michael Chabon. He has such a hyperfluent vocabulary but sometimes he would scale the language back. Some of the descriptions were comparatively plain, and that plainness contrasted in such a way as to focus the reader's attention, subtly, like a whispered secret. These were some of the most important moments in the story. So, I wrote about that."

Q: What about the creative writing aspect?

A: "During that same month's time we write a minimum of fifteen pages, either new work or significant revision. You have an independent schedule, so you have to motivate yourself. One of the nice things about the low-residency model is that it mirrors the life of a working writer. Someone who has to work for a living but who also has a separate creative life. It is a demanding schedule of work, and there is not a regularly meeting community of people to rely upon for support or an influx of creative energy during those dark moments I suspect all writers have: where the words have jaunted off without saying goodbye and haven't bothered to call or write to say when they can be expected back. You've got to figure a way to work through it on your own."

Q: What are the residencies like?

A: "They're very fun. You don't see these people for six months, so you look forward to it. The first couple of days there is a tangible excitement. It's nice to take time off from professional work. You dive into the writing life. The days are long, though. Craft and writing seminars in the morning, workshops in the afternoon, readings in the evening. That's every day. You have to pace yourself, otherwise you can wear down pretty fast. These take place on the Lesley campus in Cambridge. It's a very vibrant and literary community. There are lots of places to go, and things to do. That's both good and bad. You have more to do, but that can also undercut the community feel of the program. Groups of people can go their separate ways at night. If instead you were sequestered in the woods or at the top of a mountain and the resident and entertainment options limited, then there might be more of a sense of being together."

Q: What about the community of a low-residency program?

A: "You make friends and colleagues during the ten days of the residency. You can call them up after the residency is over, for advice or just someone to talk with about your projects. I write to a handful of people on a fairly regular basis, sometimes to talk about problems with the work, sometimes just to chat. There is also a student-run online community. A message board. There's that avenue for more wide-ranging responses."

Q: What's your daily schedule like?

A: "I'm an editorial assistant at a textbook company in downtown

Boston. The job is forty hours a week not including travel time, which, depending on the trains, is about an hour each way. It can be difficult when you come home from work. You eat, do a bit of unwinding, then you get down to your creative work."

Q: What advice would you offer to new students?
A: "The most important thing is to take a real special care in choosing your faculty and keeping in touch with them. For the six months between residencies, they are your primary link to the program. It makes a big difference, how you respond to their teaching and how they respond to your work. Before you choose, go to the library and read their work. That's tremendously helpful. Seek out those people whose work you respond to. A good mentor could be someone who simply places the right texts before you . . . Another thing is cultivating relationships with other students. It's helpful to have those relationships and to know that they are going through the same things. It's not necessary that they're in the same genre as you. Sometimes its nice to get another perspective, the same way it is to read in another genre. Those relationships can help fill gaps that the faculty can't fill or shouldn't fill . . . In a similar way, wherever you are locally, I think it's a good idea to attend readings and literary evens as much as possible. It keeps your creative energy up. You get involved with other writers and readers."

Scott McCabe is a graduate of the M.F.A. program at Lesley University and of Bowdoin College. His work has appeared in *The Harvard Review*.

YOUR TEACHING

This short section addresses questions related to teaching composition or creative writing on the university level. It may also be helpful for graduate students who are teaching or research assistants for professors.

What can you tell us about teaching?

What I'd like to tell you about teaching would take a whole other book, so I'll try to be brief here.

There will be some sort of orientation for first-time teachers, sponsored by the program, the department, or the university. Be sure to attend this, as it will be not only smart, but required. Some orientations will last a full semester before you teach or during your first teaching semester, and others will be a few days before the first semester starts.

During the orientation you'll learn about the specific goals of your courses. You'll learn about each of the assignments you'll be teaching. (For example, at the University of Massachusetts we taught a number of papers, including the personal essay, responding-to-text, the research paper, the persuasive essay, and others.) You'll learn about which tools—group exercises, homework, conferences, peer feedback, in-class writing—you'll use to meet these goals. And of course you'll talk about teaching styles and methods.

We had a good orientation at the University of Massachusetts, but *by far* the most helpful aspect of the three-day course was a one hour Q&A with veteran graduate teachers. Here, we concentrated on the nuts and bolts of running a classroom. Questions included:

- What should I include in the syllabus?
- What kind of writing exercises should I use?
- What about my attendance policy?
- How long will it take me to grade 18–25 papers?
- What kind of comments should I include?
- How will I encourage discussion in the class?
- Is this textbook useful and, if so, which sections are most useful?
- How many weeks should I plan ahead?
- How many weeks for each class paper?

And those are just the big-picture nuts and bolts. Some smaller though no less important issues are: Should my students call me Mr. Kealey or Tom? What arrangement of chairs—facing the blackboard, in a circle, in small groups—is best for which days or assignments? How do I set up a library tour? What happens when I don't know the answer to a question? What happens on a sunny day when students ask, "Can we have class outside?"

My point? Don't count on the basic orientation to teach you everything, or even to teach you what you actually need to know about running a classroom day in and day out.

I am *strongly* encouraging you to seek out veteran teachers and listen to what they have to say. Buy them coffee and ask them specific questions. Good teachers are excited about teaching, and they like to talk about it. Ask a veteran teacher if you can sit in on a class. You can learn a lot by just watching. While your solutions/ strategies in the classroom may be different, you can receive good insight from people who have been there and done that.

How can I balance teaching and writing?

Good question. When I was a graduate student, a professor once said to a group of us: "Do as little as you can, teaching wise, and concentrate on your writing instead." I didn't think much of this at the time, and I still don't. However, a necessary point arises: Make sure you schedule writing time, and don't allow your teaching responsibilities to infringe upon it. Remember that you'll spend a lot of time on your teaching during the weeks that papers/stories/poems are due. Schedule for that. And schedule more of your writing time for the other weeks.

I am strongly encouraging you to set up four to five blocks of time each week for your writing. Some people like to maintain a consistent schedule: Every morning for two hours. Or every evening, starting at 10 pm, for three hours. Or all day Saturday. Try to observe your best writing times: Some of us are morning people, others are night owls. I'm encouraging you to block out two to three hours, three times, during the weekdays, and a longer writing session sometime over the weekends. Choose the times: say, 9 pm Monday nights, 8 am Tuesdays and Thursdays, Saturday from noon to five. Stick to these times, and don't allow other aspects—teaching, personal, classwork—to infringe on them. You are in school to write. Make it a priority, and keep it a priority.

Can you give us some other tips about teaching?

- Try to avoid teaching Monday-Wednesday-Friday classes. Many schools have dropped this practice, and I'm not sure why all of them haven't. Try to get on a Monday-Wednesday schedule or a Tuesday-Thursday schedule. Why? Because it will allow more time for your writing and, more importantly, you can do more with two hour-and-a-half classes than you can with three fifty-minute classes. Why is that? Because I said so. Learn the hard way if you like.
- The syllabus: Do ask for syllabi from veteran teachers. Try to keep your syllabus to no more than two pages. Offer a brief

introduction to the class, introduce the textbook, state goals, make clear the requirements, make the attendance policy clear, and offer a brief schedule.

- Why a brief schedule? You should have a rough-draft schedule of the entire semester in your own notes. Try to stick to this. In many cases, schedules will change. I used to give students the schedule for the entire semester. Then I went to half a semester. Then I went to the first six classes. Nowadays, I simply include the first three classes on the syllabus. I always tell students what the schedule will be three classes in advance, during each class, but I allow for some leeway for classes beyond that. Be clear about requirements in your syllabus, but allow yourself some flexibility in meeting these requirements.
- I like to write the schedule for the next few classes on the board during the break in the class. This means that I've told them *and* shown them. This will save you a lot of headaches.
- Take roll at the beginning of each class. This will help you learn students' names (which you should know by the end of the second week), and it will show that you are paying attention to who is there and who is not.
- The first day of classes: I want to take attendance, pass out the syllabus, explain the syllabus, go around the room and ask them to introduce themselves in some way (be sure to ask veteran teachers about how they do this). I want to introduce the textbook, I want them to write in class in some way so that they get into the habit of writing (ask veteran teachers about writing exercises), and I want to make the homework for the next class clear. Often, I'll let them leave early on the first day, especially since they've got a lot to do around campus. However, I make it clear that we'll stay for the full class for the remainder of the semester.
- As far as classroom discussions go, don't be afraid of the silence. By that I mean: When you ask a question of the class, wait for them to answer, even if you have to wait for a full minute. Stay quiet, and someone will eventually answer. If you get into the habit of asking a question, pausing for a few seconds, then answering the question yourself, students will expect this pattern for the rest of the semester. In fact, they'll assume that this is the pattern you prefer. So, ask your questions and wait for the answers. Don't be afraid of the silence.

- If you're having trouble keeping discussions going, don't be afraid to call on students directly. Often, they are simply waiting for permission to answer.

- A break: If your class will run longer than an hour and a half, allow a five-minute break. This gives you a break too, and you can reorganize for the second half of class. It allows students to go to the bathroom or simply stretch their legs. This sounds obvious to me as I write it, but a lot of teachers don't do this. You can only cram so much information into their heads in an hour and a half. Give their brains and other body parts a break. I always start the second half exactly after five minutes. This stops five minute breaks from stretching into ten minutes. Students take note of your promptness.

- Try to accomplish three major things each class period. These might include a lecture about writing, a discussion about a text, an in-class writing assignment, small group work, or introducing a new assignment. Try to keep these to no more than twenty-five minutes each. This keeps the class period rolling along, it prevents students from getting bored, and it allows you to accomplish a lot during the course of the semester. Most importantly, it keeps you organized. And an organized teacher is an effective teacher.

- It's your job to help students improve on their writing weaknesses and to help them correct mistakes. But it's also your job to reinforce and draw attention to the things they are doing well. Make sure you do both. The second is as important as the first.

- Always allow for in-class writing time, at least once a week. This helps them practice what you're preaching. Less importantly to them, but perhaps more importantly to you, it allows blocks of time that you don't need to prepare for intensely. Find interesting writing exercises, or give them specific assignments that are relevant to or actually allow them to work on their papers.

- Get to know your fellow teachers, veterans and rookies alike. You can bounce ideas off of them, trade class plans, and perhaps most importantly, you will have people to decompress with after a long day or week of teaching. Just having people available who can commiserate with the same challenges and situations will help you a great deal. Try to schedule your office hours at the same time as other teachers. If no students visit, this can be prime teacher discussion time.

- Take care of yourself. Get your sleep, eat right, make time for yourself, your writing, your own classes. If you're healthy and happy, your classroom atmosphere will be the same.

Any final thoughts on teaching?

Everyone wants to take creative writing classes. They are often some of the most popular classes on campus, and there are often long waiting lists for students. Motivation in these classes is no problem.

On the other hand, no one wants to take composition classes. Some students believe they should've "placed out" of them, other students think writing is boring, and a good number of students believe that they are simply not good writers, and they dread going to these classes.

That sounds depressing, but that need not be the case. Look at it this way: If you can make your class fun, interesting, sometimes unpredictable, and, most importantly, relevant and useful to students, then they'll look at writing in a very different way. Their expectations are low for the class. I am *not* arguing that you should meet these low expectations. But I am saying, if you can make the class fun, challenging, and relevant to students, you'll surprise them. A lot of their friends are taking boring classes. If yours rises above their expectations, they'll take note, and you'll have their efforts and interest.

If you believe, communicate, and project that writing is valuable and important to you, then you'll have a much easier time of teaching. And when you project that *their* writing is valuable and important to you, you'll have an even easier time.

You're not necessarily *friends* with students. (And you're certainly not their enemy.) You're their teacher, guide, and mentor. But you're also a colleague of theirs, in the art and craft of writing. Be a friend of their writing, and of their class experience.

THE WRITING WORKSHOP

Aimee Bender

Q: As a teacher, what do you expect out of your students in workshop?

A: "It's important that students turn in work that they've spent some time on. That they've thought about and rewritten. It's important that they spend time analyzing the work of their peers and that they write good critiques. To be honest, I want students to make the workshop the top priority of all their classes. Ideally, graduate students will be writing as regularly as possible. Learning and keeping some sort of writing routine is important."

This section addresses the creative writing workshop. Tips here for both writers and readers.

What can you tell us about workshop?

A few things. First, the classes will hold anywhere from eight to sixteen students. Fiction and nonfiction students will be workshopped twice, while poetry students can have their work workshopped five or more times in a semester. There may be an introductory two or three classes where students read published work and discuss it, or complete short writing assignments. For the most part, however, you'll jump right into the workshop discussion.

A workshop, as I've said, is a sort of editorial meeting about student work. A professor and the other students discuss a writer's work—its strengths and weaknesses—and offer suggestions for improvement. Meanwhile, the writer sits and listens and takes notes. After, the writer can ask specific questions not covered during the workshop. Often, students and the professor will write letters to the student or make comments on the manuscript.

I have some random tips that may be of use to you:

When you are the writer:

- Never volunteer to go first. By that I mean, don't turn your story/poem into be workshopped first. Why not? Because the class is just getting to know each other, and it's not a well-oiled machine yet. The first workshop is often, though not always, a dry run for the rest of the semester. So, if you can, hold your work back till the third or fourth workshop.
- Don't write something the night before and then turn it in the next day. We've all had strokes of genius at midnight or after. But by the light of day, the genius tends to leak away.

The best writing is rewriting. So remember that a good workshop story/poem is one that has been written, has been set aside for a few days, and then is come back to with your editor's eye.

- You'll be making copies for the class *before* your workshop. Make sure you leave enough time to factor for broken copy machines, long lines, etc.
- Slackers. There are always slackers in the group who don't write letters or who offer little to no comments. If someone slacks off on my work, then I slack off on theirs. I pay attention to the writers in class who pay attention to me. Generally, I'll give my best effort the first time around, then I make changes accordingly. Keep in mind that shy or introverted students may not say much in class, but may offer outstanding and insightful written comments.
- Be a stenographer when your own writing is being workshopped. I like to write down everything, or close to everything, that is said in my workshop. I'll write a person's name and then their comment, and then on to the next person. Why? Two reasons: First, you'll have a written record of what was said. This is important, as one strong comment in class may distract you from equally or more useful earlier comments. When you have the written record, you have notes from which to work. And second, when I concentrate on writing everyone's comments down, I concentrate less on how my work is looked upon critically or negatively. This is your baby on the table, and there will be all sorts of surprising and sometimes hurtful comments. Keep your emotions out of it by writing down all comments. Concentrate on content, not criticism.
- I like to read everyone's comments the evening after my workshop. Then I set them aside for a week, let them bounce around in my head, allow my subconscious to organize them (emphasizing some, rejecting others), and then I sit down to rewrite.
- At the end of the workshop, you'll likely be given a chance to ask questions or seek clarifications. Stick to these things. Don't explain your story or offer excuses about what you were trying to do. Comments like "Well, what you guys obviously didn't see was . . ." is not helpful. Your poem or story either worked for this audience or it did not. It must stand on its own. Ask questions about areas that were not covered, or ask a specific student to expand a comment that was brushed over in the discussion.

When you are one of the readers:

- Don't be a know-it-all. You may see the goal of twenty-first century poetry/fiction/nonfiction in a clear way. Others will likely see it differently. Don't impose your aesthetic on the rest of the class. A workshop is all about the work you have before you. Work to understand what it is, and what the author is trying to achieve. Keep your comments limited within this parameter. By all means, do suggest improvements or ways of thinking that the author may not be aware of. But don't impose your style on another writer.

- In general, workshop is not about right and wrong. It's about offering options to the writer. Suggestions, not demands. So avoid personal arguments with other workshop people. Argue ideas, not personalities.

- On that note, be prepared for others to object or argue with your comments. Let them. While you may feel the need to clarify or reinforce, keep these to a minimum. This is not a courtroom. You've offered your options. If you've stated them clearly and effectively, then the writer will take note. The readers in a workshop may end up learning a lot, but remember that the workshop is primarily for the benefit of the writer.

- Don't talk to the writer. As a general rule, the writer of the work will remain silent during workshop. So, it does no good to say, "Jen, I wondered why you included this information about the mother so soon?" Instead, aim your questions and comments to the teacher or to the class as a whole.

- Don't spend time talking about grammar. A misspelling or a misuse of a word can easily be marked on the manuscript for the writer to read later. A workshop will be anywhere from ten to fifty minutes. Either way, time is precious. Stick to the structure, form, and content of the work. Offer options to the writer. If a grammar error is consistent throughout the work, then you might point it out in a short comment.

- Do offer strength assessment. Yes, you are pointing out shortcomings of the work, but it is equally important to reinforce the aspects that are working well in a story or poem. Be sure to comment on these. Often, and appropriately, strength assessment is offered at the beginning of a workshop. Typically, if the stronger aspects of a work are not praised early, then the workshop tends to forget about them.

- Letters. I always write letters in my fiction workshops. These can be hand-written, though typed is preferred. Generally, notes for shorter poetry works will be on the page of the work. The workshop leader will likely give instructions on his/her preference. In any case, be a good letter writer. Reinforce three aspects that are working well, and offer three recommendations for improvement. Spend some time on each of these aspects. When you write good letters, you'll likely receive good letters in return.

- Keep your verbal comments specific, and offer examples if possible. Keep your comments to around thirty seconds each, and no more than a minute. Be clear and concise. Writing your letter or your written comments should give you an idea of your best suggestions. Don't be afraid to give your overall impression of the work—talk about what it is and what it's trying to do—but keep the majority of your comments specific, useful, and applicable.

Any final comments about workshop?

Yes. My colleague at UMass, Nick Montemarano, used to tell me this: When you're the writer in workshop, it's like driving a car with twelve people in the backseat, all of them telling you which way to go. They all may actually be giving good directions and driving instructions, but if you listen to all of them, you're likely to crash the car. Be sure to pick out a few specific voices. Who best understands what you're trying to do with a work? Who gives the best insights? Who defends the aspects that are most dear to you? This is another good reason for not going first in a workshop. You can observe how individuals treat others' work on the table. By the end of your first year, you should have a good idea about who understands and values your work and who doesn't. Pay much more attention to the former and less to the latter.

PUBLISHING IN LITERARY MAGAZINES

This section offers insights and tips on publishing your work in literary magazines and journals.

What about publishing? Should we be submitting our work to magazines and journals?

Definitely yes. Send out work that is polished and, in your view, complete. Work that has been workshopped and edited to your satisfaction. Some tips on sending work:

- There are somewhere short of three hundred national literary magazines in the United States. They each publish some combination of fiction, poetry, essays, reviews, and artwork.

- *Writer's Market, Poets Market,* and *Novel and Short Story Market* are the three guides for researching publishing magazines. They list all magazines accepting open submissions, and they will provide submission information, advice, and addresses. Buy them and read them. They're big, so don't get overwhelmed. Plan on reading, say, ten pages at a time. Take some notes in the margins. Part of beginning the publication process is reading these books carefully, and taking notes as to which magazines might be a good fit for your work

- Look for magazines that are established and are looking for work similar to yours. Go to your local bookstore and read literary magazines. Find journals that you like, and send to those.

- One tip I've often heard: Look at the poetry books or story collections of your favorite authors. Often there are lists of magazines where the work was previously published. This is often found on the copyright or acknowledgments page. Consider these magazines for your work.

- Also, consider *The Best American Series* (stories, poetry, nonfiction, etc.). There are lists of magazines at the back of these books and citations for the work included.

- A very incomplete list, but a starting point nonetheless, is: *Story Quarterly, Poetry, Tin House, Glimmer Train, Pleiades, American Poetry Review, Southwest Review, Zyzzyva, Virginia Quarterly Review, Missouri Review, Boulevard, Puerto del Sol, Five Points, The Sun, Georgia Review, Epoch, Field, Ploughshares, Tri Quarterly Fiction, Prairie Schooner, Crazyhorse, Alaska Quarterly Review, Indiana Review, Witness, Grand Street, Iowa Review, Mid-American Review, Jubilat, Meridian, Black Warrior Review, Michigan Quarterly Review, Chicago Review, Southern Review, Fiction, Seattle Review, New England Review, Quarterly West, North American Review, Third Coast, Gulf Coast.* And some of the big ones: *Atlantic, Harper's, Paris Review, McSweeney's,* and *Zoetrope.*

- Do your research, and don't limit yourself to these. There are many fine magazines out there.
- Consult Web sites that list links to magazines. I've listed these in Appendix C.
- Consult veteran students and professors about where to send work.
- Generally speaking, magazines are looking for stories in the 3000–5000 word range. Magazines look for poetry in the one to five page range. Many publications actively seek new writers, so don't be intimidated if you haven't published before. Part of being a writer is sending your work out, getting rejected, revising your work, sending it out again, and getting it placed. If you can't stand rejection, look for another line of work. Sometimes your work is not ready; sometimes editors are idiots. Control what you can: Revise and polish your work, study the market, then send your work out. If you receive a return letter asking for revisions, then revise and resend within a month's time.
- Send one story at a time to a magazine, or three to five poems.
- The manuscript: No crazy fonts or wacky pagination. Use Times New Roman (or the like) font. No title pages. Number your pages, especially in the case of fiction. Staple or paper clip your work. Put your name on page one, and I like to put my name and e-mail address on the last page of my stories. Some magazines are notorious for losing your accompanying letter. If publishers want your poem or story, make sure they can get in contact with you.
- Of course, many magazines now accept submissions online. This is a great time and postage-saving technological advance. Magazines will normally get back to you in less time when they accept submissions online.
- Generally speaking, magazines will reply in three months time.
- Simultaneous submissions: Some magazines do not accept submissions that you've also sent elsewhere. I think this is stupid. You can't afford to send a poem out, wait three or more months (sometimes as long as six to eight months), get rejected, and then send it out again, only to wait for another half year. I avoid simultaneous submission magazines, and you should too. Some magazines say, "Simultaneous is okay, as long as you let us know, and as long as you contact us if a piece is accepted elsewhere." This seems fair to me, and you should honor that request.

- That said, how many magazines should you send one work to? My answer: around six at a time. Spread your net wide.
- And, that said, *make sure* you keep track of where and when you've sent your work. Write it down in your notebook or in a computer file. Update it as you are accepted and rejected. Don't make the mistake of sending a rejected work to the *same* magazine later.
- I've had stories that were rejected eight times by varying publishers, then accepted somewhere else. Keep sending your work. If a work is rejected, say, a dozen times, then it likely needs to be set aside and edited. You can't account for editors' tastes and opinions, but you can polish or rework your poems/stories when necessary.
- The accompanying letter: Make it formal. Include the magazine's address and your address. If at all possible, find the name of the appropriate editor and address the letter to him/her. If not, "Fiction Editor," or the like, will do. Don't explain your poem or story. If you have previous publications, list them in your letter. If you are in a writing program, state it. Before I was published, I simply wrote "Here's a story," and I was accepted at a number of places. Be direct and brief. Your work has to stand on its own. Before you send out your first letter, show it to someone who has had success in getting published. Follow his or her advice.
- Other advice: When sending via post (snail mail), always, always, always include a Self-Addressed Stamped Envelope (SASE).
- Sometimes you get paid, sometimes you don't. I've been paid as much as $500 and as little as two copies of the magazine. You're trying to get your work and your name out there for people to see. Don't worry about the money.
- I'd say that I've sent about 120 copies (total) of around twenty original stories. Twelve of my stories were accepted. That means about 10 percent of the time I've dropped something in the mail, it's been taken. It also means that 90 percent of the time, the work has not been accepted. That's manageable for me, and seems—give or take a few percentage points—what my colleagues have experienced as well. My point? Expect to be rejected, and keep sending. One work placed for ten sent out is workable. Often, the majority of rejections will come as you first send your work.
- Keep sending. Persistence and patience counts for everything in the writing world.

"Counterpoint:
A Guide to the MFA and Beyond from an Outsider Who Became an Insider"

Adam Johnson

OKAY, LET'S SAY you've got a fresh, well-earned bachelor's degree, and what you'd like to do is get an M.F.A. in creative writing. As an undergraduate, you took some great writing courses, pestered your writing teachers during their office hours, and threw a party in which everyone dressed as his or her favorite literary figure. You hung out with the writers in workshops who "got" your work and fell in love with books that blew you away. There were lots of survey courses, spread across other cultures and centuries, and you became a more thoughtful critic and better human being for all that reading. For a few years, you wrote and read all the time, you worked out and did yoga every day, and found your share of romance. So, with the sun setting on the last season of intramural softball, as the whir of the margarita blender begins to fade, you set your sights on what's ahead: graduate school and the prospects of turning the thing you love into a way of life.

Well, as someone who has an M.A., an M.F.A. and a Ph.D., I have three initial pieces of advice.

First off, don't do it. Writing is full of heartache, struggle, and poverty, and because we live in unreaderly times, few people will appreciate you and what you do. More people will read the Unabomber's "Manifesto" than the literature you or I produce. Plus, you spend all your time alone in a dark room in your sweatpants, and there's nothing healthy about that lifestyle. There are many new growth industries that need smart young people like yourself. Have you considered a career in prison administration? Do you know how much a military contract consultant makes? You could retire at thirty-eight and *then* become a writer.

If you insist on becoming a writer (and I don't feel bad steering people away from the life because if anyone—*anyone*, a mother, boyfriend, parole officer—can talk you out of your dream, well, it wasn't meant to be), do it for the right reasons. It's hard to catalog all the wrong reasons for getting an M.F.A., but here are a few. If you want to get an M.F.A. because, after your bachelor's degree, you're lost, lazy or unsure, well, after an M.F.A., you'll soon be back in the same boat. People get M.F.A.s for other equally lame reasons: to avoid paying student loans, to continue qualifying for a trust fund, or to avoid mandatory military service in the nation of your birth. Well, maybe avoiding military service in the nation of your birth isn't such a bad reason to get an M.F.A. I must admit that, when applying for M.F.A. programs, I visualized myself in the air-conditioning for a couple years.

Second, the worst reason to get an M.F.A. is to avoid real life. The whole reason to learn to write is so you'll have the skills to tell an important story, once you've lived it. Also, if you haven't lived, there's a danger that you might come to believe that an M.F.A. program *is* real life. Any graduate degree involves lots of work and self-sacrifice, but in general, you'll be breathing rarified air for a couple years. Being in an M.F.A. is like living in a sci-fi biosphere on an alien planet, where everyone shares your obscure visionary notions: namely, that literature matters, that English professors know more than other people, that typing, alone, in a library, is what everyone should be doing on a Friday night. Better to tell strangers that speaking Klingon is what turns you on.

The easiest solution to this scenario is to get out in the world a live a little. Before you head off for that master's degree, I suggest you hitch up with the Immigration Service as a border patrol agent. Sign a year contract. After twelve weeks of intensive training in Yuma, Arizona, you'll be assigned to jeweltowns like Sierra Vista or Calexico. Before you know it, you'll be rolling old school in a mint green blazer uplinked to a Blackhawk helicopter that will do your bidding. You'll have night vision goggles, infrared trackers, and, before you know it, you'll be pointing your Mag-Lite across the arroyo at another living, breathing human being. You lock eyes, and I tell you, greenhorn, there's a whole novel in that a moment. Plus you get benefits and vacation. Okay, okay, I'm from Arizona, so I'm partial to jobs that include pistols and Big Gulps. The point is that poetry and fiction are composed of images and details. Authority comes from experience, and the definition of a good image or detail is that thing you couldn't make up, that observation that had to be witnessed and reported, the thing the reader believes *couldn't* be concocted. You need to train your eye to observe these before you can become proficient at concocting them.

I suppose firearms aren't necessary to get real-life details. A job as a restaurant inspector will do, even the vainglorious EMT position. Have you considered delivering oxygen tanks? The job doesn't matter as long as you come in contact with real people in situations where something's at stake.

If you're going to take a couple years off between your undergraduate and graduate degrees for the express purpose of "living life," I suggest you work, rather than traveling to Prague to live on Marlboros and Sangaria, let alone joining the Peace Corps. If you're looking to simply take notes on your fellow humans, sit on a bench in the mall. Work is about labor and locomotion, about personal industry, about taking a position within a larger system. If you work, avoid selling things and be leery of all-consuming jobs like cruise-shipping. Steer clear of taking jobs where others recreate; it's easy to come under the spell that you, too, are having fun. This rules out bars, hotels, casinos, ski slopes, and so on. Most jobs that come with a uniform are safe. Carry a clipboard. Buy a thermos. Pack your lunch.

Third, the reason *to* get an M.F.A. is the most noble and the most selfish: That you adore writing, and you know that you'd never regret dedicating a couple years of your life to the thing about which you are most passionate. This conception of an M.F.A. is based on service, that you want to live in servitude of this mysterious thing called writing that's taken hold of your heart. Basically, it's deciding to live the writer's life temporarily in the hopes that it becomes permanent. This means writing every day, devouring books, drafting, listening to the advice of others, and taking risks with your work. And of course there's a professional dimension. I've been emphasizing the importance of knowing the working world before you undertake an M.F.A., because it's a tremendous amount of work. To earn your degree, you'll be asked to complete a book-length project, which will require deadlines, late nights, word counts, and timelines. And don't forget: you'll be balancing teaching, graduate courses, and your thesis. It may seem that all this work is adversarial to living the writer's life, but teaching writing and studying writing at least elucidate and inspire. And it's controlled adversity, applied with the hope that you'll thrive in its face. (As opposed to trying to live the writer's life while you frame houses during the day and bartend at night.)

The other noble reason to seek an M.F.A. is to enlist a mentor. As an undergraduate, you get small connections with instructors, usually lasting no more than a semester or two. I advocate to my undergraduate writing students that they take as many different writing instructors as possible so they can become familiar with the range of insightful response to their work. For a graduate student, it's just the opposite. The point of seeking an M.F.A. is to apprentice yourself to a writer you admire. By taking you on as a protégé, the writer agrees to make you a year-long personal project, reading everything that you write, in the hopes of personally charting the growth of your voice. In return, you treat this mentor like a god.

This is a rare and special relationship, one that exists in precious few places outside the American university. There's simply no other socially acceptable way to establish a relationship with writers, aside from stalking their laundromats or ambushing them outside their therapists' offices. Send your favorite writer a fan letter and you'll probably get a nice, brief note in response. Send your favorite writer a 600-page handwritten novel and see what happens. Forget about asking that writer to read everything you compose for a couple years. When you ask a stranger for that kind of commitment, you're asking for a relationship and, generally, asking strangers for extended relationships ends in moments of tenderness like a chemical spray or a court-ordered evaluation. So it is to the English department that you must go to commandeer the time of a writer who's actually written a body of work. The first meeting with your mentor in the English department mailroom is likely to be just as awkward as on the street, but remember: here the writer (now a professor) is getting 401k benefits to talk to you. It's a perfect match, as there are few ways for writers to make a living beyond the fat of a state-run bureaucracy, and most writers I've met have amazing stories of their own mentorship by other writers. Successful writers are looking for ways to give back. The M.F.A. program allows all this to happen.

There was no book like this when I went off to pursue a writer's life. I'd been a lame student in high school, one whose motto was "Cs get degrees." I soon became a shoring carpenter, and my path in the few years it took me to get to college was pocked with bridges, pump stations, and midrises. My lone literary influence during this time was a millwright who lived in his van in the parking lot of a chemical plant we were building in Chandler, Arizona. He wrote haiku all day and kept a pistol-gripped, sawed-off shotgun in his toolbox, each barrel of which was loaded with a half roll of dimes—for "crowd disbursement," he said. I only remember one of his haikus:

Oh, the cry of the
cricket, caught in the hawk's beak.
I hammer my thumb.

And a couple years later I was working on the eighth deck of the Scottsdale Hilton when I had one of my two epiphanies so far in life. Gerry, the tower crane operator, liked to eat KFC all day long at the controls. He was an expert at how wind and speed and gravity exerted themselves in the space below him, so he could toss a drumstick from the boomhouse with wicked accuracy, and, with twenty stories to freefall, incredible velocity. The decks, as we built them, were marked with large grease stains of his near misses. One day I was crossing the freshly cured concrete deck with a worm-drive Skilsaw in my hand, daydreaming about something or other. Then my knees went out from under me. It was as if a great fist had come down. The impact scored a deep red line on my forehead from the hard hat webbing, and as I dusted myself off and pieced things together, it was like I was a character in a bad novel: "Adam Johnson rose from the hardened plane, and shaking his fist at the sky, let the world know he was headed to college where he would sit in the air-conditioning all day." Of course I didn't quit for a few more months—that's how epiphanies really work—time enough to see a tragic accident unfold on the job site: Gerry, instead of climbing down and up twenty flights of stairs every time he needed to use the bathroom, urinated in a gallon milk jug, which he kept on the boom of the crane—out in the Arizona sun. An emergency braking maneuver shook the jug off the crane, launching a hot urine bomb that, when it detonated hundreds of feet below, nearly killed a man. The incident ended with a pistol.

My second epiphany came when I was in a fiction writing class at Arizona State University. I'd made it to college, but was an older student, and not a very good one. I excelled at easy courses, including History of Music, Jazz Influences, and Family Studies, which you watched once a week on TV. Finally, a friend told me that creative writing was the easiest A on campus. That's how I found myself in the class of Ron Carlson, one of this generation's marquee practitioners of the short story. Suddenly, all the "flaws" I'd been told

I'd had—daydreaming, lying, rubbernecking, exaggeration—all combined to make something good: a short story, which was technically a work of art, and in my art appreciation class, it was made clear to us that creating art was like the highest, most lasting thing a person could do. I was hooked.

I began writing short stories at night, where I worked as a doorman at a nightclub. Summers, I kept a notepad in my toolbelt and took notes with a square carpenter's pencil. I pioneered a writing technique by which stories were composed on legal pads while driving at high speeds across the Sonoran Desert. The theory was that the conscious mind, occupied with steering and so on, would free the darkest part of my soul to emerge on the page. Yes, I'd been reading Conrad, and I never solved the serious penmanship issues that came with drive-writing. My roommates were getting worried; I'd head off to my room to write when it was obvious that a keg had just been tapped. My girlfriend didn't "get" my stories. She had to go.

For all my ambition, it was hard to produce satisfying work. My writing wasn't good, wouldn't be for a while, mind you. I just knew it could be better, but I didn't know how, and I was left unsatisfied, especially when I began working full time. I was trying, but failing to thrive. I felt like Dante did when he strayed from the path and encountered the She-Wolf of Incontinence. What Dante needed was Virgil.

For me, wanting an M.F.A. was a no-brainer. I didn't have fantasies of being a literary star—I just wanted to live the life, to be in the game. I wanted to commune with other writers as well. There were cool writers at ASU, but M.F.A. students don't tend to hang out with undergrads, and my fellow undergrads looked at me with suspicion: I was older, wore workboots to class, and it was obvious I'd never seen a Kurosawa movie. Okay, I also had a mullet haircut. And maybe I had some hygiene issues.

I applied to ten schools and was accepted to six, including one that was supposed to be the best. Honestly, my applications were shots in the dark. I'd never even been to some of the states where the programs were, let alone know of the writers who taught at them. I asked people's opinions, but only became less sure of choices based on rumor and suggestion. Fretting about my decision, people consoled me with lines like "If writing is what you love, you'll be happy any where you end up." But I didn't want to be happy. I wanted to be a better writer. I wanted to learn new skills, to be challenged by my peers, to have a mentor help me make "that leap" everyone was talking about.

I called one M.F.A. program and got the name of a current student; he supposed his program was "pretty cool" but he sounded a little aloof and noncommittal. He used the word "ameliorate," which I had to look up. Wouldn't the M.F.A. program give me the name of their most excited student? Was he a reason to rule that program out? I had no way of knowing. I found a cheap plane ticket and flew to the East Coast to meet with the director of another M.F.A. program. I had a six-hour turnaround, so I rented a car, drove to the university, and: the director didn't show up. I sat alone in an English department hallway for two hours and then flew home. That *was* a reason to rule a program out.

Where was *this* book when I needed it?

At the time, I was reading a collection of short stories by Robert Olen Butler. It was called *A Good Scent from a Strange Mountain*, and it was to win the Pulitzer Prize later in the year. I was in love with the stories, all written in the first person with the kind of heart and voice that I was striving for. Butler's bio said he taught at a small M.F.A. program in Louisiana named McNeese State, and I noticed the book's dedication was to another teacher in the M.F.A. program, a good sign, I thought. I called the program, and they gave me Butler's home phone number. Butler said to send him a story, and the next week he called me back with a response to my work that changed the way I saw my own writing.

This brings me to my main piece of advice for all prospectors of graduate programs, be they M.A., M.F.A. or Ph.D.: seek a mentor. Is Tim O'Brien your biggest influence? Do you love George Saunders? Do you want to be Lorrie Moore? These writers are all currently teaching at M.F.A. programs. Don't worry so much about a program's reputation, geography, and entrance requirements. Make a list of the writers you admire and discover where they teach. Make contact, if possible. Then, grail-like, seek your mentor.

Of course none of this will happen if you don't get into grad school. So do well on your GREs. Get good letters of recommendation. Polish a story that shows off all your skills. Then apply to lots of programs that you'd consider attending. You'll get into some percentage of them, and some will seem more appealing than others, based on tuition waivers, teaching stipends, even fellowships perhaps. All of that matters. What I'm suggesting is that once you have choices, understand that the human connection is the most important factor, in my opinion, in making your final decision. I know many writers who hold M.F.A. degrees. When they recollect the first years they dedicated themselves to their art, I never hear them say, *I went to Iowa—the money was awesome!* Or *The student teaching at Irvine changed my life!* Invariably, I hear writers speak of teachers that made a difference, great peers, meeting visiting writers at parties, discovering new books, and artistic growth. And of that list, besides perhaps the parties, the only element you can control as a prospective student is picking a teacher who seems to want to make a difference.

I ended up going to McNeese State, a three-year program that conferred both an M.A. and an M.F.A. It was the right decision. Butler was a visionary teacher with a unified field theory of how literary fiction worked, and honestly, I don't know how a person could settle into the writer's life and begin to form a relationship with his or her work in less than three-years. It took me a year to truly absorb the ideas I was exposed to, and another year to put them into practice. By the end of my second year, I was writing competent stories, a couple of which were published, that had little to do with me. It was in my last year that I made the leap I'd been hoping for: I began writing a different kind of story, one in which I felt spookily exposed on the page. I'd finally managed to merge what I cared about with what a narrator cared about, creating a character that was of me and apart from me, that allowed me to recognize myself and still make discoveries.

Then disaster struck. I graduated. I actually earned my M.F.A. and was out on my ass just when I wanted nothing more than to redouble my writing efforts. My dream of being a daily, working writer was slipping away. Sure, I could go back to the kinds of jobs I had before, but my productivity was going to plummet. I found myself fantasizing about situations that would give me unlimited time to write. Perhaps I could read instruments at an Antarctic research facility. Wasn't there some brainwave experiment that needed a volunteer to live in a cave for a year? I literally had a dream in which I was on the space station Mir: I had a frustrating time eating the powdered food and urinating into the plastic tube, but floating through the capsule were all these beautiful space-age pens, more than I could ever use. Yes, I was cracking up; quickly, I began applying for Ph.D. programs.

This post-M.F.A. option has become increasingly popular in the past decade for just these reasons. Namely, that a writer with some ability and some promise has little recourse in the world. If you work full time, your art is in constant danger of becoming a hobby, or worse, a diverting escape. Writers, unfortunately, are valued about as much as harpsichordists today and, like harpsichordists, they find support under the conservatory auspices of the university. That said, in your transition to life as working writer, the Ph.D. is a nice middle step: still structured and supportive, but much more independent.

Completing the M.F.A., you've hopefully had a mentor and an environment where you take risks with form and subject matter. You've had a community that helped you figure things out and let you know when you hit the mark (and when you didn't.) After the M.F.A., you need support more than mentorship, time more than feedback and independence more than supervision, so you'll have the freedom to undertake bigger projects.

I applied to six Ph.D. programs and was accepted to four. But, as with my M.F.A., I found my way more through a person than an application. I'd been a big fan of *Writing Fiction*, probably the smartest book out there on narrative technique. It was written by Janet Burroway, who taught at Florida State University in Tallahassee. That's where I went, and Burroway became my major professor, directing a dissertation that I eventually published under the title *Emporium*. While an M.F.A. mentor is often like a seasoned platoon commander who keeps you on mission, a Ph.D. mentor is someone you seek out when you need advice, like an oracle who watches over you and dispenses wisdom just when you need it.

As a Ph.D. student, you're on your way, rather than finding it, yet you haven't arrived, as your professors have. It can be a strange middle ground. Your writing gets workshopped harder than the master's students' work and, because you've been at this longer, you're expected to publish and succeed. On the other hand, it seemed to me that the Ph.D. students got the lion's share of recognition, financial support, and good classes to teach. That's something to think about if you're heading off to a program that hosts master's and doctoral students side by side.

Finally, while it's possible to see an M.F.A. as a couple year vacation to the beloved isles of writing, the Ph.D. will take you at least four years to complete, and it's hard not to see parallels with the monastery. First, there's the vow of poverty that you're basically taking. And don't forget the purgatorial architecture of your typical English building. You've got to read a lot of obscure texts and fulfill a translation requirement. And of course, there's blind devotion, angry questioning, and hopefully, a vision or two.

While there's an element of play theory to the M.F.A., the Ph.D. requires more serious survival skills. Here are some that I recommend: Feel no shame about stealing toilet paper from the faculty bathroom. Guilt your parents into buying you an ergonomic chair. Attend all reading receptions with baggies in your pockets so you can load up on cheese cubes and boiled shrimp. Get some reading glasses, and have your eyes checked regularly. In times of crisis, avail yourself of the six free psychotherapy sessions most universities provide. Steal the copy machine codes from all of your peers and slip all your fiction submissions into the English department mail cart. Know that carpel tunnel braces, while far from being sporty, can be sexy in a kind of fetish sort of way, so go for the model with the black leather webbing. Keep at least two stories in the mail to six different publications at all time. Go to half the parties, attend all the readings, and write twice as much as everyone else. Never forget that you're living your dream, something most people would kill for.

And what did I do when I finished my Ph.D.? I began applying for fellowships.

Adam Johnson holds the M.F.A. from McNeese State University and the Ph.D. from Florida State University. He currently teaches at Stanford University, where he was a Wallace Stegner Fellow and Jones Lecturer. His works include the novel *Parasites Like Us* and the story collection *Emporium*. His fiction has appeared in *Esquire, Harper's, Paris Review*, as well as *Best New American Voices*.

APPENDIX A

Interviews

Of course, you've seen short quotes from these program directors, professors, and students throughout the book. I thought it would be helpful to include the remainder of the interviews here. Many important insights and opinions come from these writers.

Aimee Bender is a professor of English at the University of Southern California. She received the M.F.A. in fiction from the University of California Irvine. Her works include *The Girl in the Flammable Skirt* and *An Invisible Sign of My Own*. Her fiction has also appeared in the *Pushcart Prize*, *McSweeney's*, *Harpers*, and the *Paris Review*.

Q: Did your writing change during your graduate years, and if so, in what way?
A: "Yes, it's true that my writing changed. I was encouraged to write more fairy-tale-like things, and that was incredibly liberating for me. That encouragement came from both the professors and the other writers in the workshop. I remember watching everyone else's work change. We talked a lot in workshop about the fallback position, a writing place that is too safe. Writing what is reliable. But if you feel supported, you can push past that fallback position and do something different. I remember one colleague whose novel was so different from his short stories. It was a radical and beautiful thing . . . We were given the expectation that each of us could write even better than we already were. There was a sense that there was a higher

131

standard. As a teacher I aspire to that now. The bar that I hold up for my students comes from a desire to help them make their writing more than it is, and more than they think it could be."

Q: From the point of view of a graduate student, how important is teaching experience to a writer's experience?
A: "They are definitely separate from each other. I don't think the teaching is necessarily helpful to the work of writer. Teaching is helpful for teaching experience. Some people I've known are overwhelmed by the time commitment. To me, it's a parallel interest. I like teaching and I like writing, but they're separate. Teaching helps remind me what's important in writing, so in that way it's useful, but it's not the only way to be reminded of that . . . Of course, an important aspect of teaching is that you get money for it. That's important to anyone."

Q: How do you, as a committee member, weigh the different aspects of the Ph.D. application?
A: "I read the creative sample first. Then the critical sample and the personal statement. The creative sample is the major factor, but we'll talk about the whole package. The GRE scores round out the picture. If we're looking for amazing in one area, it's the creative work."

Q: What do teachers want for and from their students?
A: "That's a good question. I want them to become more particular, more distinct in their work. I want them to go deep and to take risks. I want to give them a protected space so they can do these things. I want to encourage those risks. I want them to have funding. I want them to have as much time as they can. From them, I want motivation and a commitment to the workshop. I want them to have some sense of what they're doing, but I want an open mind too. Sometimes graduate students come in thinking they already know what they want to do. It's a tricky balance, to be open to learning. You have to be both open-minded and stubborn. You want your writing to change. Change is exciting. You have to be open to breaking your writing apart, and then stubborn about putting it back together the way you want."

Tracy K. Smith is a professor of English at the University of Pittsburgh. She received her M.F.A. from Columbia University

and was a Wallace Stegner Fellow at Stanford University. *The Body's Question* is her first book of poetry, and her work has appeared in *Poetry 30, Poetry Daily, Callaloo, The Nebraska Review, Gulf Coast*, and elsewhere.

Q: How important was "place" in your selection of a graduate program?

A: "One of the big benefits for me, in New York City, was the vital literary scene. On any given night you could choose from a variety of readings and even participate in some of them. I met people inside the program, I met people outside of the program. I'd encourage students to consider whether there will be a community outside of their program. When you're a student, so much hinges on the courses you take in your particular field, but your work ought also to be based on everything that happens to and interests you as a person. Everything impacts you in some way. New York reminded me of that, and gave me more material to grapple with."

Q: Where should a student "be" in his or her writing career when applying to graduate programs?

A: "It varies. You can learn something valuable at different stages of your life. My one year off from college gave me renewed vigor toward learning. I'd dive into my assignments. People who come straight out of college can arrive at grad school with a sense of continuity. And people with years off from school have new material to grapple with. It depends most on the desire you have for writing. It's more of a question of what's going on for you and the necessity that your work is based on. It depends more on your inner world than the outside world."

Q: Can you talk about what students should and should not expect from a graduate program?

A: "I think that the big thing students shouldn't necessarily expect is a career. You go in thinking that you're automatically going to get a teaching position and a book when you graduate with an M.F.A., but in reality, it's a much longer road than that. What's more important is the idea of community and friendship with people who are interested in the same things. You're seeking a set of readers whom you trust with your work. You're looking for new directions in which to read. You want mentors and faculty who can see what you're striving toward. I thought I'd be the kid at twenty-five who comes out of grad school with a book. Instead, I had to develop more devotion to writing, more commitment. The M.F.A. environment and the time afterward created a sense of necessity for me as a poet."

Q: Where does funding fit into criteria?
A: "Ideally I would make my list of schools based on place and the people teaching there. Then I would make a realistic choice based on what I could afford. I went into a lot of debt, and that might be a little crazy. But I got so much out of my experience in an M.F.A. program that I don't regret it. There are other ways to approach funding. One person I went to school with had a Jacob Javits Fellowship, so he was funded from outside the university. Exploring all of those options is a wise idea. My advice? Make funding as much of a factor as it needs to be."

Q: Any advice on the workshop experience?
A: "I have an extreme regret for workshops where people feel the need to display the knowledge they have under their belt by breaking down other writers. It happens, I think, because of their own insecurity, their own need for status. It's hard on the person being ripped to shreds, but it's also hard on the person who is aggressive in that way. We had a person like that in my incoming class at Columbia, and all he did was create a quick exit for himself from our community. He missed out on the support we gave one another. He was not part of what the rest of us were. It's important to listen to what each poet's work seems to be striving toward. Listen to what the voice is based on and what the poet is interested in. Guide your comments in that direction. If you can find a way of empathizing with that, of stepping inside it, even if it's detached from what you're used to, it broadens your own sense of possibilities. I think a workshop is most helpful when that generosity is available."

Q: How does teaching experience fit with the graduate experience?
A: "There's always something good about it. When you teach while you're young, you get a sense of whether or not teaching is ultimately what you want to do. I don't think it's absolutely imperative, though. If you want to teach, the M.F.A., even without teaching experience, makes you a good candidate for teaching creative writing or even composition. Sometimes waiting a little longer to teach can be helpful. Waiting a little while before becoming a teacher gave me time to clarify and develop the ideas that were important to me

as a student, and test them, try them on, before I had to formulate them into a specific set of teaching tools. I could explore more. Another thing to remember is: Teaching is not restricted to the college level. You can get valuable experience out in the community working with younger or older populations."

George Saunders is a professor of creative writing at Syracuse University, where he was also an M.F.A. student in fiction. His works include *Pastoralia*, *CivilWarLand in Bad Decline*, and *The Very Persistent Gappers of Frip*. His fiction has appeared in *The New Yorker*, *Harper's*, *Story*, and many other publications. He has twice won the National Magazine Award for fiction.

Q: How important is a third year of an M.F.A. program?
A: "I think it's really important. There seems to be a cycle I've noticed. In the first year, students are sizing things up. Some of them wonder if they're good enough to belong in a program. In the second year, there's usually some drama. It may be anything from workshop hostility to simply being overloaded with graduate work. But in the third year, the writing gets done. It's almost as if the first two years, you spend figuring out how to be a writer. Then in the third year, you actually do it . . . I'm definitely a big advocate of the third year. You don't want to be pushed out the door just as you're getting comfortable."

Q: Advice on choosing work for the writing sample?
A: "The most common answer is 'Send your best work.' And though that is the answer, I know it's not very helpful. If it was my kid, I'd remind him that the reading period is a compressed time for faculty. We've got two weeks to read these manuscripts, six hours a day. Sorry, I don't normally read six hours a day, so it's a tough two weeks. So put your best work first. If you've got four great pages of poetry or four great pages of fiction, put those first. It's like a reality show, pitching yourself to the audience, or the girl, or the panel, or the guy in the suit. You don't have an hour. I would put the best four pages first."

Q: How much do letters of recommendation influence the committee?
A: "For the first couple of picks, we don't really worry about the letters. We feel that, if we really like the writing, the rest will take care of

itself. So, you find out your number one choice is, per a letter of rec, a homicidal murderer. Well, our feeling might be: Maybe that's okay, maybe we can work with that, we can get him a little portable jail cell, whatever. For the rest, we really only look at them if it's a close call—two equally matched writers, and we can't decide. Then we try to see who might be, say, more adaptable, or who might be the harder worker. My advice is to choose three people who are going to say nice things about you, and don't worry too much about finding big names. Mostly, these letters are a way for our committee to enjoy ourselves once we make the picks. We say, 'Look, we did the right thing! Look at this letter!'"

Q: What if a student is not accepted anywhere? What advice would you offer? Should a student apply again the next year?
A: "Yes, I'd say you definitely apply again. Not necessarily to the same programs. To some different ones, and maybe the two or three that you really wanted to go to. I look at my own writing in my twenties, when one year I was writing very poorly and the next year I got suddenly, mysteriously better. Progress seems to happen in surges. You have to shake things up. You should get feedback on your writing, maybe take a class, definitely work on new samples for the next round. My feeling is, acceptance to an M.F.A. program is not diagnostic in either direction. People who turn out to be great writers could be rejected, and people who turn out to be poor writers could be accepted. There are so many unknowns: How long has a writer been working on their portfolio? How old are they? Where are they in their developmental arc? I think a good deal of humility is in order in every direction. Teachers should be unsure of their own powers of selection, and writers should be humble, and hopeful, about their ability to transform their own work, suddenly, unexpectedly . . . I sense that some applicants don't read much. We get a lot of TV stories. If you've been rejected, one way to shake things up is to question your reading list. Find writing that is new to you. Two or three writers that you're really excited about. Follow their lineage back. Know everything about them. Immerse yourself in those writers. For me, it was Stuart Dybek. He was from Chicago like me. Reading him, I suddenly understood the unique power of truly contemporary literature. I felt things I hadn't ever felt before while reading. That was empowering and exciting. The thing is, if this is going to be your life, you have to go at it with everything you've got. This may be the great hidden blessing of being in an M.F.A.

program: You see that being a writer is not so rare. The deeply personal question becomes: Which writer are you going to be?"

Q: Advice on making the most of a program?
A: "Two things. First, it's not high school. It's not about the social thing, or about getting your due from the higher-ups. It's not about pleasing your teacher or competing with your classmates. It's about finding your voice and getting your writing done. Second, be assertive about getting what you need from professors. We lay a lot of resources at students' feet, but we don't place those resources *on* their feet. It's not like they're in Paris in the 1920s, and Gertrude Stein is going to take them to lunch and make their careers. What I mean is, the writer has to be creative and assertive about making sure that whatever they need, they get. Everyone keeps office hours. The more serious students use them. They come in and ask questions about craft or whatever's bothering them or that they're excited about. Seek mentoring. You're in charge of your resources. Think of a creative writing program as a kind of artistic petri dish. Your job is to open your mind up and let everything in, trying not to be too judgmental. If great advice comes from a bogus, or drunken, or self-righteous, or little-published source, take it anyway."

Rachel Kadish teaches in the M.F.A. program at Lesley University and is a graduate of the M.A. program in creative writing at New York University. Her novels include *From a Sealed Room* and *Soon Also for You*. She is recipient of a National Endowment for the Arts Fellowship and the Koret Award for a Young Writer on Jewish Themes. Her work has also appeared in *Best American Short Stories* and *The Pushcart Prize*.

Q: Can you explain the teacher/student interaction in your low-residency experience?
A: "I write very detailed comments on their stories and responses. The student writes responses to what he or she has read. We stick to the plan. Or, we change it, but we both agree on this. I might say, 'I see you've taken a different turn in your writing, so let's start something new now, or revise, or try these readings.' It's a very flexible form of teaching. You can tailor the assignments for each student. I work with four students each semester. One of the things I

like is that we can pivot on a dime if we choose. That's hard to do in a class of twelve or twenty."

Q: What criteria should students use in selecting an M.F.A. program?
A: "There are two that are important to me personally. The funding issue is, I think, a prerequisite. I personally don't believe in going into debt to go to a creative writing graduate school. It's not like an M.B.A. You won't necessarily earn the money back in the two years after school, and you don't want to obligate yourself to taking a post-M.F.A. job that won't allow you to write. So I tend to counsel people to not go into debt. Having said that, the most important thing for me is faculty. Don't just look at the list of faculty, but call up the program and find out who will actually *be there* during those years. They might list your favorite writer, but he or she may have only taught there for one year. Find out about the faculty you'll get to work with. Some of the best teachers I've had were not such big names at the time. You go to the library and scan their novels and see if you want to learn from this person."

Q: What about your experience in choosing a program?
A: "I guess my experience was not normal. I was living overseas at the time, not sure what I was going to do. I was dating someone who could only live in three cities: New York, Los Angeles, and Cincinnati. I only applied to two graduate programs and two Ph.D. programs. I chose NYU because location-wise it worked, and because I'd always wanted to be a graduate student in New York City. Of course, I broke up with the guy before the summer was over. But New York University worked well for me."

Q: What advice would you offer for "getting the writing done"?
A: "You definitely have to power through it. You need to know what works for you. I need structure, and deadlines. I create deadlines, even artificial ones. I promise something to someone for a certain date. It's important to me to promise it to someone I'm a little intimidated by, or who I don't want to let down. My friend who will say "Oh, take all the time you need" is a good friend, but he or she is not the ideal deadline person. It's helpful to me to be a little intimidated. That's just how I work . . . Part of me appreciates the hard-ass response on that. You either get it done or you do not. I see my time differently now that I have kids. I don't answer the phone when I'm working. I don't take breaks. I don't meet another writer

for coffee. You write because it makes you tick, and you write in whatever way is most effective for you. But at the end of the day I'm left with the hard-ass response: No one is going to do it for you."

Q: What overall advice would you offer to graduate students in creative writing?
A: "I feel the need to remind people that it's not an M.B.A. or a law degree. You're growing as a writer. You're taking the degree to work on your art. You're writing within an incubator for a few years. Learn as much as you possibly can, and pick up some skills in writing, editing, and teaching. But don't put that financial pressure on yourself that you have to have the academic job or book contract in hand. Try not to set yourself up in a financial situation so that you have to have a concrete result on the other side. Keep your debts low so that you have freedom to continue your writing."

Q: Do you have any observations on the workshop experience?
A: "There can be some ego-bruising in workshop. That's unfortunately part of the experience. No one comes out completely unscathed. Just remember, you're learning to write for the rest of your life, so look at workshop as an important part, but just a small part of that life. Feedback is important, but not all of it is always in the best interest of the writer. You want to find one or two sympatico readers and one or two sympatico faculty. That alone is a triumph and can make a program a wonderful experience. Everything else, you get through and observe. Don't get thrown if your first workshop is not geared to the writing you like. There's the baseball analogy: Getting a hit one in three times is a very good percentage."

Victoria Chang holds an M.F.A. from Warren Wilson College, and she is currently a Ph.D. candidate at the University of Southern California. She also holds degrees from Stanford University and the University of Michigan, and works for Stanford as a business researcher and writer. Her first book of poetry is *Circle*, and she is editor of the anthology *Asian American Poetry: The Next Generation*.

Q: Like a lot of writers, you work in the business world by day, and you write creatively by night. What advice can you offer postgraduates about keeping writing a priority?

A: "Yes, I am straddling two worlds. I write for a living, but it's a different kind of writing than poetry. I might eventually like to teach, though. As a writer you need to know your tolerance for living close to the poverty level. I'm probably less comfortable with it than most writers for a variety of reasons, familial and cultural pressures included. It's important to me to have a consistent income. But other people can find their own balance—it's up to the individual. For me, poetry/writing and other fields are not mutually exclusive. I think sometimes people assume that if you're not teaching writing, then you're not a writer. That's ridiculous. I have a pen, just like the next person. Society looks at you strangely when you say you're a poet. That's part of the deal, but you'd be surprised at how many of my non-poet friends are interested in reading my poetry. They're just not familiar with contemporary poetry."

Q: What are the advantages and disadvantages of a low-residency program?
A: "On the downside, it's a tough experience. You don't always get teaching training, depending on what program you're in. You're not physically near people. You lose out on a lot of interactions that residency students do receive. And the ten to twelve days you spend there twice a year are really intense. On the other hand, you get a great amount of attention from a mentor. It would be difficult for me to completely articulate how well I know my professors. You learn to write letters, which is a lost art, and you develop a deep relationship with your teachers. They were focused on me and maybe two other students each semester. That's a lot of attention. In some ways, you find a life mentor in addition to a writing mentor. I learned about craft for certain. But I also learned a lot about myself because of the close observations and feedback of my teachers. In addition, at low-residency programs you have a guaranteed new teacher every semester, so if things don't work out too well, you can always count on a new teacher. This isn't always the case at residency programs."

Q: What are the differences between low-residency and residency programs?
A: "One thing to remember is that in a residency workshop, you spend the majority of class time working on other people's poems. In a low-residency program you concentrate on your own work.

And, in many ways, you have more say over what you'll study. At many low-residency programs, you design your own curriculum."

Q: Do you have any advice about negotiating with programs about funding?
A: "State your needs and concerns. Be clear. Don't offer ultimatums, but state your individual situation. Be communicative and be open, especially once you get in. Don't assume that people know your needs. Not many people are mind readers."

Q: Thoughts on the M.F.A. and Ph.D. degrees?
A: "I view the M.F.A. as an artistic degree where you learn craft. Same thing with the Ph.D. in creative writing. The Ph.D. is more about learning how to be a scholar, though. I love learning. The fact of the matter is, there are things I don't know and, even more importantly, there are things I don't know that I don't know. I want to find out what those are. Curiosity is a big aspect of being a writer. My degrees in writing are furthering my own art. I'm a firm believer that critical work is deeply embedded in the creative."

Q: What advice would you offer about workshop?
A: "It's important to work within the contract of the writer within a workshop, to critique within the writer's intentions and vision. You're not trying to make his or her work like your work. It's key to understand what the poem is doing, or trying to do, and then you can help within that framework. Our society can be so polarized, and we see things in terms of black and white, or red and blue. We give the thumbs up or thumbs down. Literature is more complex than that, and workshop should be too. Sometimes the most helpful feedback is to simply point out a writer's tendencies and proclivities. Helping a writer identify what it is he or she does, that's very important."

Heather McHugh is a teacher and writer-in-residence at the University of Washington. She is also a regular summer faculty member at the Warren Wilson College for Writers. Her many works include *Hinge & Sign*, *The Father of the Predicaments*, and translations of *101 Poems by Paul Celan* and Euripides' *Cyclops*. She is the recipient of fellowships from the National Endowment

**for the Arts, The Guggenheim Foundation, and the American
Academy of Arts and Sciences.**

Q: Why should a student be interested in a creative writing graduate degree?
A: "In my humble opinion, one of the chief virtues of a writing program is that it buys you time to focus exclusively on your reading
and writing. It is time that is formally acknowledged by the rest of
the world, and that includes parents, spouses, and friends. It is time
bought, not stolen."

Q: What criteria should students use in selecting programs?
A: "Two criteria would matter most to me, were I a student applying now for a residential M.F.A. program. First, my respect for the
writing of the faculty in residence. And second, my wish to reside at
least for a few years in the geographical setting. This second element
may matter more to me than to other people. I have to love the place
where I live. It is a crucial factor in my daily equanimity."

Q: What about researching low-residency programs?
A: "I'd look at the age and venerability of the program and its academic
seriousness. Does it rubber-stamp its students? Does it accept too high
a proportion of its applicants? Get the scuttlebutt. One would want the
most selective and most academically serious program that one could
get into. The low-residency mode is easy to turn into a year-long
replica of the lesser writers' conferences: those that mean escape from
rather than application of high standards. I'd contact the alumni or
reunion association, former students, and ask questions about these
particular issues. See how enthusiastic its alumni seem about their
time in the program and their continuing contacts with it."

Q: Advice on the writing sample?
A: "Don't add drawings of flowers or unicorns. Don't indulge in a
lot of fancy fonts. Don't think that imitating the work of the admitting faculty will greaten your chances. Featuring your own writing's
characteristic strengths is the only way to greaten your chances. But
of course, if you already know what those are and how to feature
them, you may not need an M.F.A. program."

Q: Any advice for "getting the writing done"?
A: "If you have to ask yourself how to get writing done, you probably

aren't destined to be a writer. Make yourself a good reader and count your blessings."

Q: What do students do, post-graduation? What variety of choices do students make in their post-graduate careers?
A: "I don't think post-graduate careers are usually matters of choice. Fate is the greater determiner. Most M.F.A. graduates will not go on to teach in M.F.A. programs. Some will, but not most. Publication will be more likely to avail in that regard. If your only ambition is to get a job teaching in an M.F.A. program, I'd say save your money and get yourself some prestigious publications and pray."

Michael Collier is professor and co-director of the Creative Writing Program at the University of Maryland. He is a graduate of the M.F.A. program at Arizona University. His works include *The Ledge, The Neighbor, The Folded Heart, The Clasp,* **and, as co-editor,** *The New Bread Loaf Anthology of Contemporary American Poetry.*

Q: Can you comment on the artistic vs. professional degree?
A: "An M.F.A. is not meant to professionalize you as a writer. Rather, it is an opportunity to live as fully as possible in a community of writers for two to three years. The problem with looking at an M.F.A. program as a professional degree is that it creates enormous distractions from concentrating on creating and establishing a discipline and identity as a writer."

Q: How important is location to a prospective student's criteria?
A: "I think location is important, but not as important as other things. You can become happy and interested in a wide range of locales, especially if the program is challenging. I think students discover more about a program by understanding who the faculty are. Do they publish actively? Or were their last books published twenty years ago? I agree that it's difficult to know about the quality of teaching, but that's why students should seek this information in particular. The way to do that is to talk with students who are currently in the program."

Q: What questions should prospective students ask of current students?

A: "It's very important to figure out what the teaching atmosphere is like. Do students see teachers on a regular basis? Do teachers have an open door? How are students and student work handled? If you want good access to faculty, as mentors and fellow writers, then you need to know if access is available."

Johanna Foster is a graduate student in the creative writing program at Trinity College in Dublin, Ireland.

Q: You looked at programs both in and outside the United States. Why?
A: "I've found that being abroad has always been powerful for me. You see life differently when you're abroad. You're more observant about people. You can't take things for granted. You get to look at language in a completely different way. You notice the language and all its quirks in greater detail. All the things that are new: These things stimulate my writing."

Q: During your research, what were some turn-offs from programs?
A: "Arrogance. I liked it when programs seemed confident about themselves. But there was often this sense—on the Web site, from information sessions, from administrative people and students— that their program was not only one of the best, it was better than all the rest. Some students would talk bad about other programs. 'Where else are you applying? Really? Well, they're not very good.' I would think, 'Thanks for insulting my decision-making process' . . . In the information sessions, sometimes there was this sense: Not that 'We're a better program, and we'd like to have you,' but instead, 'We're a better program, and we thought you should know that.' That was a real turn-off. If it was meant to be a deterrent, it definitely worked."

Q: Anything else?
A: "Yes, programs that were not realistic about funding. They'd say, 'You shouldn't let finances prevent you from participating in this program.' To be honest, I'd think, 'You shouldn't let this tuition prevent me from participating in this program.' Or, sometimes they were simply not forthcoming with information. Be upfront about how much it costs, and what our chances are for funding."

Q: Turn-ons?

A: "Student enthusiasm. Students who were really excited about their programs. They'd light up, talking about it. Students at Brown went out of their way. I met them through unofficial channels, through a friend, so maybe that changed things. Still, they would answer my e-mails, they'd send me invitations to readings. And it's not like Brown doesn't get enough applications. But their students seemed very dedicated to the program, and very dedicated to making it approachable."

Q: Why do you think this is the right time for a creative writing degree?

A: "To be totally honest, I wonder if it is. I thought it was. I still think it is, but I wonder. I want feedback. I want the company of other writers. I want people to read my work without my having to bake them a cake. I'm worried about when I shift my whole attention to writing. Before, it was an escape and was wonderful; now, it will be the main thing. I have a lot of self-doubt now. Is this so great because before I was doing accounting? What will I have learned when I go back to the workplace? It's tough, but at this point I'm excited about Dublin, and I'm excited about the program. People talked with a glow when they spoke about their time in the program. They said: 'That was the best year ever.' I guess I hope that is the case for me."

Bruce Snider is a Jones Lecturer in Poetry at Stanford University, where he was also a Wallace Stegner Fellow. He holds the M.F.A. in poetry and playwriting from The University of Texas Michener Center, where he later served as graduate coordinator for admissions and advising. His first book of poetry is *The Year We Studied Women*.

Q: How important is location when choosing programs?

A: "Where you're going to live is important. There are enough stresses for a writer without being miserable about your living situation. It comes down to personal preference and temperament. For me, being gay, I wanted to know if there was any kind of gay community near or at the schools. Any kind of minority community. I didn't want to live in a conservative think-tank somewhere. That mattered to me."

Q: How should students choose classes?
A: "Always talk with other students. Some programs have more flexibility in their degree plans than others. If you can take classes outside the department, take something that feeds into your work in some way. Maybe history or political science. I took a lot of film classes. Italian film, Eastern European film. I learned about how narratives are constructed visually. Also, take writing classes outside your genre. That's important. I was a poet but took fiction classes, which was very helpful. It gives you a better sense of the tools you have to work with in your particular genre, as well as the ones you don't . . . If you have a third year and the degree plan is flexible enough, take something that'll give you another outlet. Piano, drawing, something social. One student I know took a furniture-making class. He loved it. When he was struggling with his novel, he'd go to the shop and work with his hands. He solved a lot of his writing problems while building his mother a dresser."

Q: Any advice on bargaining or negotiating with programs about funding?
A: "One thing to keep in mind is that for the programs who fund all their students equally, there is nothing to bargain. Everyone gets the same thing. Otherwise, you can talk about the cost of living in that particular area. People do sometimes improve their offers by asking, but you need to be diplomatic in your approach. It's not a job offer. You should have a certain degree of modesty. Don't assume you're in some power position. No matter how good you are, you're just one person being admitted in one particular year. If you're reasonable and explain your needs, though, most programs will do what they can for you, within the bounds of their own resources."

Q: Is a third year important?
A: "Yes, I think slightly longer programs work to the student's advantage. If you're working up a manuscript, that third year makes a big difference. In some two-year programs, students sometimes feel they've spent much of that time just getting settled. In a three-year program you get two years of study and workshop, then a final year to really work on the book. That extra year gives you a chance to put together what you've learned during the previous two."

Q: Anything to avoid with the writing sample?
A: "Basic, silly things. Don't bind your sample, don't in any way try to make it attractive with pictures, photos, drawings. Don't play with the fonts. If we received something in a binder, we threw the binder away, because we put the manuscripts into a file. You'd be surprised at how many strange things we'd get. People would bind their work into a book to make it look more 'professional.' That has the opposite effect."

Q: How important is the personal statement to the committee?
A: "The truth is the bulk of the decision is based on your writing sample, but sometimes the statement makes a difference, especially in competitive programs where the committee has to make some fine distinctions between applicants. Occasionally it helps you, but more often it hurts. Don't try to be too clever, and don't try to suck up to the faculty, and whatever you do, don't come across as arrogant. The committee can be very sensitive to these things. They'll have to work for two or three-years with whomever they admit, so attitude factors in, particularly in smaller programs where's there's often less buffer between students and faculty. Be fairly direct. The committee wants to know if you're going to add something to the community, and if that something will be positive. On a very basic level, they'll want to know if you play well with others."

Q: Any overall advice on making the most of the graduate experience?
A: "No matter where you go, you can make something of it. As with most things, you can make a decision that you'll have a miserable time or an enjoyable time. You've got these two or three-years to really make the most of your writing. Attend every event you can. Read everything you can. Get to know your fellow classmates. Some of these people will go on to become important readers for you even after you leave. I always found that students who took time off before they went to graduate school really appreciated it more. You know you don't always have that kind of time . . . Also, use it as a time to take risks with your work. Often students are too product oriented. It's okay to turn something in to workshop that's an experiment, as long as you've really worked on it. The point is to become a better writer. Don't shy away from criticism. A graduate program is the place to really challenge yourself, while you have all these readers willing to tell you what they think. When you get out in the

real world, editors and reviewers are not necessarily constructive. If run properly, a writing program should be."

Peter Turchi directs the M.F.A. program for writers at Warren Wilson College. He is the author of four books, including *Maps of the Imagination: The Writer as Cartographer*, *The Girls Next Door*, and *Magician*. He is co-editor of *The Story Behind the Story: 26 Stories by Contemporary Writers and How They Work* and *Bringing the Devil to His Knees: The Craft of Fiction and the Writing Life*.

Q: What considerations should students have when researching a low-residency program?
A: "Low-residency programs typically offer a low student-to-faculty ratio, but the prospective student should learn not just how many students each faculty member will be working with but exactly what sort of relationship students have with their supervisors: how much work the supervisors read, how they respond to it, what sort of guidance is provided for the student's reading, etc. Do the supervisors also teach at the residency? Do students have access to other faculty at the residency? What are the opportunities for individual conferences? What sort of counseling or guidance is offered by an advisor or administrator? How is the student's work toward the degree evaluated, and how often? What are the degree requirements? . . . Many low-residency programs look similar on the surface (just as the description of most workshops look similar); they are distinguished by how they are executed. With that in mind, prospective students should talk to current students and alumni and even, if possible, visit a residency. They might also ask how the program maintains contact with its alumni, and what alumni services are offered."

Q: How about for programs in general?
A: "Any student applying to a graduate program in creative writing should think about what he or she most wants from the program. Ideally, first on the list will be developing the tools to become a better writer (as opposed to, say, getting a book contract). If being trained to teach creative writing (or composition), being trained to work as an editor, or some other related skill is also important to the student, that will help to narrow the list of suitable programs."

Q: Advice for low-residency students?
A: "I'm not sure the advice for low-residency students is all that different from the advice for a residential one: Devote yourself to the work; read broadly and deeply; experiment; and learn as much as possible from your reading, from your fellow students and their writing, and from the faculty, without getting distracted by opportunities for publication and awards, minor contradictions, negative criticism, self-doubt, despair, and other matters of ego. Low-residency students may have to work harder to overcome shyness during the residencies, so as to have face-to-face discussions with students and faculty, and they should also maintain phone or e-mail contact with some of the other students. There's no secret to success, though; hard work is repaid."

Q: Thoughts on your M.F.A. experience?
A: "I earned my M.F.A. at the University of Arizona, where I also had a teaching assistantship. In those days TAs taught two sections of composition every semester; as a result, I felt more like a composition instructor than a writer. That changed toward the end of my time there, as I got to teach creative writing, but the teaching load certainly detracted from the experience. On the other hand, I've had work as a teacher ever since, so I certainly got something from it . . . Strange as this may sound, and with all respect to the people who tried to teach me, I'm not sure I developed much as a writer while I was at Arizona. I learned a few important lessons, but it took a long time for them to take effect. Perhaps the most influential part of the experience was the interaction with other student writers, many of whom are still colleagues and friends today."

Q: What do teachers want for and from their students?
A: "I'll speak for myself: I hope my students will be inspired, gain a better understanding of what fiction can be and how individual pieces of fiction work, and see and implement new possibilities for their own work. Ideally, the student will have an impressive combination of talent, intelligence, enthusiasm, curiosity, dedication, conscientiousness, and perseverance. A sense of humor and decency is a bonus."

Padma Viswanathan is a graduate student in the M.F.A. fiction program at the University of Arizona. She holds an M.A. degree

in creative writing from Johns Hopkins University, and is currently at work on a historical novel set in south India, tentatively titled *Thangam*. Previous works include the plays *House of Sacred Cows*, *Disco Does Not Suck*, and *By Air, By Water, By Wood*. She is also a freelance journalist.

Q: What are the advantages and disadvantages of attending small or large programs?

A: "I'm still in touch with my classmates from Johns Hopkins. In a smaller program you'll work with the same people during a substantial arc of your and their development. My experience is, the better you get to know someone, the better responder you can be to their work. I guess the downside of a smaller program is that one very aggressive or even crazy person can spoil it for everyone. I didn't have that experience at all at Hopkins. But I'd expect that one person can really turn the workshop dynamic on its head . . . For larger programs, on a very basic level, there are more people, and that might increase your chances of finding literary kindred spirits."

Q: Should students change their criteria when it comes to decision time?

A: "I felt like my criteria were the same. Except that the discussions I had with students—I spoke with three from each program—clarified whether the program met those criteria. You definitely get a feel for the teachers, the other students, the resources, and the culture."

Q: Thoughts on teaching experience as a graduate student?

A: "Teaching composition has taught me how to teach composition. I wanted teaching experience, and that was one reason I went to an M.F.A. program. But teaching literature as a part of a creative writing course makes me a better writer, as does reading good work by classmates. And being in workshop *is* teacher training. You're practicing how to teach."

Q: Thoughts on workshop and literature classes?

A: "I do think the best way to learn how to write is through close reading of excellent writing. This is one reason I, like many people, have some reservations about the workshop process as a way of teaching writers. It's strange to me when people take two workshops per semester and then don't do much of the reading in their literature classes. That seems wrong to me."

Maria Hummel is currently a Wallace Stegner Fellow in poetry at Stanford University. She received her M.F.A. in creative writing from the University of North Carolina at Greensboro. She is author of the novel *Wilderness Run*.

Q: What is a helpful mindset for graduate students?
A: "One of the greatest things I learned from my fellow classmates was that this was a time to experiment. It was not a time to narrow down what my idea of a poem was. It was a time to broaden that idea. I had to open myself to as many styles and writers as possible. My advice is to go in with an open mind. This is a time to splash paint all over the walls and see what happens."

Q: What *shouldn't* students expect from a creative writing graduate program?
A: "It's not going to be the golden road to a published book. I remember talking with someone a few years back who said, 'I already know how to write, so I just want to go where the professors are famous. I just need their connections to get my book published.' That's wrongheaded. You shouldn't go unless you've got something to learn."

Q: Thoughts on motivation?
A: "You shouldn't expect that anyone is going to persuade you to love your writing and keep you going at it. It always comes down to your own self-motivation. You can certainly get a lot of support and feedback in a program, but no one outside of yourself is going to make you become a writer."

Q: What did you learn from working as a teaching assistant?
A: "I was a teaching assistant for Fred Chappell in a modern poetry class. I didn't actually have many responsibilities outside of teaching when he was away on book tour and grading papers. Fred is an old master of the lecture, and in class I'd sit and listen to him and take copious notes. I still pull out those notes whenever I have to instruct on someone like Auden or Kipling. It was a useful experience: watching a professor lead a room, but not being a student in the class. Not only did I hear his insights, but I got to observe how to teach."

Q: What about life after a graduate program?
A: "As long as I'm writing every day, as long as I make that appointment with myself, I feel like a writer. It doesn't matter what job I have, as long as I'm writing for some period of time. It's also important to keep up with a community as best you can. Keep up with your classmates, and try to build new networks wherever you next move . . . It's a little strange: when I published a novel several years after the program, I started to lose my identity as a poet. None of my current friends were poets. They were fiction writers, journalists, screenwriters. Then I made a friend who was a poet, and when we started having conversations about poetry, it was like coming back from another country and remembering my native tongue again. For so long, I'd only been having those conversations with myself."

Geoffrey Wolff is the director of the graduate fiction program at the University of California Irvine. He is the author of four works of nonfiction, including *The Art of Burning Bridges*, *Black Sun*, and *The Duke of Deception*, and six novels, most recently *The Age of Consent*. He is recipient of the Award in Literature from the American Academy of Arts and Letters.

Q: What is a helpful mindset for creative writing graduate students?
A: "I think principally to keep their eyes on the near term, not the long run. Gazing afar at publication rather than squinting at composition is inevitably blinding. If students will pay close attention to what's in front of them, they'll leave as better writers and certainly as better readers. Much of writing is a kind of long-haul trucking. Learning how long it takes to get better can be a rude surprise. Stamina and character are as important as natural talent."

Q: Any dangers with letters of recommendation?
A: "Applicants are at the mercy of their recommenders. They need three letters, and it's not uncommon for some endorsers not to write the letters they've agreed to write. Maybe they forget. Maybe they can't think of anything nice to say. Inasmuch as these letters are often sent directly to the schools, the applicant may be left in the dark about an incomplete file. On the other side, we frequently

receive such careful and passionately encouraging endorsements that the students who have provoked such enthusiasm would be touched to see them. You want to ask people who know you, yes. And you want to ask people you can count on."

Q: How important is funding to a student's experience?
A: "It can be a problem in many programs. You have two people in workshop: One has a tuition waiver and a $20,000 stipend; another pays full tuition of $35,000. They each bring a story or poem into workshop. It's difficult for students not to look at the work and think 'This story is $55,000 better than this other story?' At UCI (The University of California Irvine) we insist on subtracting financial competition from the cultural equation. Our bedrock principle is that what one person gets is what everyone gets. This has a benign effect on morale."

Q: What if a student is not accepted anywhere? What advice would you offer?
A: "I look at the writing I was doing as an undergraduate. I wouldn't have come within a country mile of being accepted to UCI. I was pretentious, and I was trying to make music. Some people develop very slowly. I think most writers know when they've turned a corner. They know something has happened. For others, they pursue the M.F.A. because their best grades in undergraduate were in creative writing classes. Well, good grades are cheap in undergraduate creative writing classes. That's not enough. Someone who is serious will be addicted to reading, and be able to display the fruits of that passion in his or her application . . . Finally, the failure of a piece of work or an application is not prophetic. Repeated often enough it can be, but it's not necessarily so. Writing is an accumulation of failures until—maybe, no guarantee—you begin to get it right."

Q: What's important in a workshop setting?
A: "Stability is important in a workshop. The class must have integrity. This begins with the instructor but radiates through the group. Stability enables candor. If good will is assumed, you don't have to be hesitant in giving or receiving judgments. Really, a program's determining factor is the good character and intelligence of its colleagues. Once a program begins to draw good students, they recruit one another."

Quotes used in this work also from:

Steve Almond is a graduate of the M.F.A. program at the University of North Carolina Greensboro, and he teaches creative writing at Boston College. His works include *The Evil B.B. Chow*, *Candyfreak*, *My Life in Heavy Metal*, and the forthcoming *Which Brings Me to You: A Novel in Confessions*.

Thomas E. Kennedy teaches in the M.F.A. program at Fairleigh Dickinson University, and he is a graduate of the M.F.A. program at Vermont College. His many works include the novels *Kerrigan's Copenhagen*, *Unreal City*, and *Crossing Borders*, the story collections *Murphy's Angel* and *Drive, Dive, Dance & Fight*, and books about writing, including *Realism & Other Illusions: Essays on the Craft of Fiction*.

APPENDIX B

Reading Lists

AT ONE POINT I'D CREATED A LIST OF NOVELS, nonfiction books, poetry books, craft books, etc. to include here, but I found this too prescriptive. Who to leave on? Who to leave off? What sorts of styles are being promoted here? I felt that such a list would become a bit of a lightning rod of criticism for *this* book (writers and friends of writers can be a touchy sort), and the integrity of this book and its contents is important to me. That said, I've included here links to reading lists compiled by various individuals, organizations, and programs.

The reading lists of the Gotham Writers Workshop, in particular, are as impressive, comprehensive, and updated as any lists I've found on the Web. There are terrific subcategories in each genre that include the actual creative works, books about craft, anthologies, periodicals, reference, and era. Definitely worth a visit by any prospective student or reader.

A reading list in just about every genre. Updated and comprehensive. From **The Gotham Writers Workshop**—
http://www.writingclasses.com/WritersResources/resources.php

The **Arizona State University English Department** list in poetry, fiction, and playwriting. Links are on the bottom right, in tiny font—
http://www.asu.edu/creativewriting/rdglists/

The **University of North Carolina Wilmington M.F.A. Program** reading list in fiction, poetry, creative nonfiction, and playwriting. This is a PDF file—
http://www.uncwil.edu/writers/documents/MFAreadinglist.pdf

Sue William Silverman offers one of the best nonfiction reading lists anywhere. From the University of Iowa Nonfiction page—
http://www.english.uiowa.edu/nonfiction/readinglist.html

The University of Alaska Fairbanks reading lists in poetry, fiction, and nonfiction—
http://www.uaf.edu/english/degreesoffered/compind.html

Bruce Dobler of the University of Pittsburgh offers a list for creative nonfiction—
http://www.pitt.edu/~bdobler/brieflist.html

The San Jose State University M.F.A. program reading list in fiction, poetry, creative nonfiction, and playwriting—
http://www2. sjsu.edu/depts/english/MFA/reading_list.html

Lighthouse has a terrific site for screenwriters, with links to many other sites—
http://www.lighthouse.org.uk/pages/film_and_video/networks_an d_links/projects/Screenwriting.php

The University of St. Louis undergraduate reading lists in fiction and poetry—
http://www.umsl.edu/divisions/artscience/english/creative/readinglist.html

The Brooklyn College M.F.A. program reading list in fiction, playwriting, and poetry—
http://depthome.brooklyn.cuny.edu/english/graduate/mfa/r_list.htm

The Western Illinois theatre department offers a list for the M.F.A. in theatre—
http://www.wiu.edu/theatre/mfaexamreadinglist.shtml

William Ronald Craig of MovieMind has a list of how-to books on screenwriting—
http://www.screenwritinghelp.com/bMoMind-ReadList.html

APPENDIX C

Helpful Sources Online

As of Summer 2005, these sites were up and running.

ORGANIZATIONS

The **Associated Writing Programs** is an organization that supports writers and writing organizations around the world. They publish the very helpful *AWP Official Guide to Writing Programs*—
http://awpwriter.org

Poets and Writers.org has long been a terrific resource for beginning and seasoned writers. The site and magazine contains information about fellowships, colonies, publications . . . you name it. One of the most important resources for writers—
http://www.pw.org/

Poets and Writers also lists most of the writing programs in the country—
http://www.pw.org/links_pages/Writing_Programs/

If you create a username and password, you can get access to the **Poets and Writers Message Boards**, which include topics on M.F.A. programs—
http://www.pw.org/speak.htm

The **Modern Language Association** promotes the study and teaching of language and literature at universities—
http://www.mla.org/homepage

LISTINGS AND RANKINGS

For a listing of the **U.S. News and World Report 1997 Rankings** (thanks to Albert Rouzie)—
http://www-as.phy.ohiou.edu/~rouzie/569A/compcreative/University.htm

Web Del Sol has a Creative Writing Project, linking surfers to specific programs and universities—
http://webdelsol.com/CWP/

Fictionweek has also included many of the rankings—
http://www.fictionweek.com/univwrite.html

Zoo Press has listings and links to many of the writing programs in the country—
http://www.zoopress.org/poetry/programs.html

For whatever it's worth in regard to creative writing programs, here is the *U.S. News and World Report* **Rankings of America's Best Colleges**—
http://www.usnews.com/usnews/edu/college/rankings/brief/natudoc/tier1/t1natudoc_brief.php

GradSchools.com lists many programs by region—
http://www.gradschools.com/programs/creative_writing.html

A listing of **Graduate Schools outside the U.S.** with creative writing programs—
http://www.gradschools.com/listings/out/creative_write_out.html

Drowning Man has a comprehensive list of literary publications—
http://www.drowningman.net/

The Nebraska Center for Writers includes information on programs in state and across the country, as well as a helpful links section—
http://mockingbird.creighton.edu/NCW/cwp.htm

ADVICE

Grand Valley State Department of Writing has an outstanding resource page of links and advice. If you go nowhere else, go here—
http://www.gvsu.edu/writing/cw_resources.htm

Angela Jane Fountas answers a few M.F.A. questions on the Seattle Writer Grrls site—
http://www.seattlewritergrrls.org/archive/2001i3_mfahelp.htm

And Jane's main Web site, **Write Habit**, is an excellent resource for a variety of writing questions and answers—
http://www.writehabit.org/

Tips on applying to an M.F.A. program in creative writing, from **eSSORTMENT**—
http://mn.essortment.com/applicationmast_rvze.htm

A basic overview of M.F.A. programs, from the **Princeton Review**—
http://www.princetonreview.com/grad/research/programProfiles/basicinfo.asp?programID=49

Suzanne Keen has written a terrific article about English literature graduate programs.—
http://english.wlu.edu/program/gradschool.htm

. . . as has **Linda Troost**
http://english.wlu.edu/program/gradschool.htm

Daniel Green discusses creative writing and literary study in RE:AL—
http://libweb.sfasu.edu/real/vol28-2/notmerelyacad.htm

Lucinda Roy of Virginia Tech has created a PowerPoint slide show about the business of writing. This is a PDF site—
http://www.english.vt.edu/~roy/NewWWW/WritingBusiness.pdf

The University of Oregon has the best FAQ page I've seen from programs. Though many questions are UofO specific, many are not—
http://darkwing.uoregon.edu/~crwrweb/faq.htm

American Book Publishing has a helpful article titled "Is an M.F.A. Program Right for You?"—
http://www.american-book.com/Articles/aredvargus2.htm

Joseph Schuster looks at the academic marketplace regarding creative writing programs—
http://www.webster.edu/~schustjm/creative.htm

Linda Formichelli writes about the M.F.A. application process—
http://www.gvsu.edu/writing/cw_resources.htm

Kevin Clark offers advice for potential M.F.A. students—
http://cla.calpoly.edu/~kclark/mfaqa.html

Erika Dreifus offers the "Lowdown on Low-Residency Programs."
From *Poets and Writers*—
http://www.pw.org/mag/0503/dreifus.htm

The Writers House and Career Services at University of Penn sent
out a questionnaire about writing programs to graduate students and faculty. Nine people responded, and their insightful comments are here—
http://www.vpul.upenn.edu/careerservices/gradprof/grad/gradmfa_
writing.htm

Ann Emmert Abbott discusses M.F.A. programs—
http://www.writersdigest.com/articles/abbott_dreams.asp

AWP has an "Advice for Writers" page with links—
http://awpwriter.org/careers/articles.htm

The University of Washington has both advice and links for students interested in M.F.A.s in creative writing or M.A.s/Ph.Ds in
English Literature—
http://depts.washington.edu/engl/advising/gradschool/grad-
choose.html#MFA

CRITIQUES

Jason Sanford looks at short shorts and the M.F.A. degree at
Story South—
http://www.storysouth.com/fall2004/shortshorts.html

Briggs Seekins's essay on the poetry M.F.A. is much talked about
on the Web—
http://www.cosmoetica.com/D4-BS1.htm

Sarah Gold looks back on her M.F.A. degree at Salon.com—
http://archive.salon.com/it/

Laura Miller wonders about fiction programs for Salon.com—
http://www.salon.com/april97/writing970401.html

BLOGS ABOUT WRITING

Moby Lives—
http://mobylives.com/

Maud Newton—
http://maudnewton.com/blog/

Bookslut—
http://www.bookslut.com/

The Elegant Variation—
http://marksarvas.blogs.com/elegvar/

Beatrice—
http://beatrice.com/

The Moorish Girl is an excellent literary blog in its own right, and
it also has a link page to other literary blogs—
http://www.moorishgirl.com/

OTHER

Financial Aid. George Mason University has a very good page for
national financial aid resources. Scroll down to the bottom of the
page—
http://creativewriting.gmu.edu/apply/financial_assistance.html

For listings of poetry book contests, visit **The Poetry Society of
America**—
http://www.poetrysociety.org/psa-links.php

ZooPress.org also has contest listings, in poetry and fiction.

The **University of Massachusetts** has listing of film schools,
including those that feature screenwriting—
http://www.umass.edu/film/focus.html

Poetry Daily. One new poem every day. A great site—
http://www.poems.com/

Poewar.com has an eclectic mix of writing-related links—
http://poewar.com/articles/

FASA. The Application for Federal Student Aid—
http://www.fafsa.ed.gov/

Jacob Javits Fellowship. A national fellowship for graduate students—
http://www.ed.gov/programs/jacobjavits/index.html

The University of Minnesota lists post-graduate fellowships and opportunities—
http://english.cla.umn.edu/creativewriting/announcements/jobs.html

The UCLA Writers Program is one of the best extension and distance learning programs in the country—
http://www.uclaextension.edu/

Shaw Guides provides listings of writers conferences and workshops—
http://writing.shawguides.com/

List of Writing Programs

I'VE WORKED HARD to make this a complete and up-to-date list of creative writing programs at the master's and doctorate levels. Prospective students should take note of the "type" of program: whether the degree has a focus on creative writing or on literature with an emphasis/track/thesis in creative writing. If basic information was easily available on a Web site, then it is included here. I would encourage program directors to read the end of chapter 3 for more information about what details to include on a Web site in an accessible way.

In the interest of space and accuracy, I decided not to include other information about faculty, specific requirements outside the degree hours, and application deadlines and advice. Why? Because these things are subject to change, and I want this handbook to be as accurate as possible. I would encourage potential students to use the basic information here concerning location, genre, degree, length of program, and type of program to narrow an initial search, and then to visit the Web sites of their programs of interest to find more specific and up-to-date information.

The programs are divided into four groups: Master's Programs in the United States, Ph.D. programs in the United States, Low-Residency Master's Programs, and Graduate Writing Programs outside the United States. I hope this decision will prove to be the most easily navigated for prospective students.

To say that I received a great deal of help from undergraduate students at Stanford in this section and other sections would be a complete understatement. Fourteen students gave generously of their time and talents in order to collect and organize the following information. In many cases, they found additional information that, for the above-mentioned reason, I decided not to include. Very special thanks to Carolyn Abrams, Jennifer Carr, Max Doty, Karen

English, Anthony Ha, Jessica Goldman, Jennifer Kong, Jack Loveridge, Karan Mahajan, Nik Sawe, Andy Orrin, Devmin Palihakkara, Camille Ricketts, and Jenny Zhang, for all of their work and help. Though the information contained here seems basic, the successful search of simple facts, especially on many, many confusing Web sites, was no small task. And the organization and interpretation of facts was oftentimes more difficult still. My students saved me (and you, the reader) hours and hours of time by sacrificing hours and hours of theirs. Thank you again.

The checking of the facts in this section was left to me, and any errors are mine.

MASTER'S PROGRAMS IN CREATIVE WRITING

ALABAMA

University of Alabama, Birmingham
Birmingham, Alabama
http://www.uab.edu/english/grad/concw.html
M.A. in English with a concentration in creative writing. Two years (30 degree hours), in fiction, creative nonfiction, or poetry.

University of Alabama, Tuscaloosa
Tuscaloosa, Alabama
http://www.bama.ua.edu/~writing
M.F.A., three to four years (48 degree hours), in digital media, nonfiction, screenwriting, autobiography, poetry, and fiction.
Other: "It's our policy to accept only applicants to whom we can pledge financial support for the duration of their programs."

Auburn University
Auburn, Alabama
http://www.auburn.edu/english/gs/handbook/index.htm
M.A. in English with creative writing concentration. Two years (24 degree hours).

University of South Alabama
Mobile, Alabama
http://www.southalabama.edu/english/graduate.html
M.A. in English with concentration in creative writing, in fiction, nonfiction, or poetry. Two years (36 degree hours).

ALASKA

University of Alaska, Anchorage
Anchorage, Alaska

http://cwla.uaa.alaska.edu/MFAinfo.htm
M.F.A., two to three years (45 degree hours, and there is a part-time option),
in creative nonfiction, fiction, poetry, and drama for stage and screen.
Other: Approximately sixty students attend the program.

University of Alaska, Fairbanks
Fairbanks, Alaska
http://www.uaf.edu/english/
M.F.A., two years (45 degree hours), in fiction, nonfiction, and poetry.

ARIZONA

Arizona State University Tempe
Tempe, Arizona
http://www.asu.edu/clas/english/gradstudies/mfa.htm
M.F.A., two to three years (48 degree hours), in poetry, fiction, or playwriting.
Other: The playwriting concentration is 60 degree hours.

University of Arizona Tucson
Tucson, Arizona
http://cwp.web.arizona.edu/
M.F.A., two or more years (36 degree hours), in fiction, poetry, and creative
nonfiction.
Other: Part-time study is possible.

Northern Arizona University
Flagstaff, Arizona
http://www.nau.edu/english/cw/creative.html
M.A. in English with a creative writing emphasis, in poetry or fiction. Two
years (36 degree hours).

ARKANSAS

University of Arkansas, Fayetteville
Fayetteville, Arkansas
http://www.uark.edu/depts/english/PCWT.html
M.F.A., three years (60 degree hours) in poetry, fiction, screenwriting, or
creative nonfiction.

CALIFORNIA

University of California Davis
Davis, California
http://www.english.ucdavis.edu/req_MA.htm
M.A. in creative writing. Two years (36 degree hours) in fiction, nonfiction
or poetry.

University of California Irvine
Irvine, California
http://www.humanities.uci.edu/english/creativewriting/index.html
M.F.A., two years, in fiction and poetry.
Note: Approximately ten students accepted each year . . . "All students normally receive some form of financial assistance, and all students receive in-service training in university-level teaching."

University of California Riverside
Riverside, California
http://www.students.ucr.edu/catalog/current/crwtgp.html
M.F.A., three years, in creative writing and writing for the performing arts.
Note: "Offers writers the ability to move fluidly within various arenas of creative writing, including the genres of poetry, fiction, nonfiction, play-writing, and screenwriting, as well as in multimedia studies."

Chapman University
Orange, California
http://www1.chapman.edu/catalog/current/grad/sca.html#MFACW
English page: http://www.chapman.edu/sca/english/
M.F.A., three or more years (60 degree hours).
Note: Don't expect much help from these Web sites.

California College of the Arts
San Francisco and Oakland, California
http://www.cca.edu/academics/creativewriting/index.php
M.F.A., four years, in fiction, poetry, creative nonfiction, and playwriting.
Note: Very much an interdisciplinary program, with required courses in drawing, media history, and a community service internship.

California Institute of the Arts
Valencia, California
http://www.calarts.edu/~writing/
M.F.A., two years (44 degree hours), with concentrations in cultural commentary, new fiction, experimental criticism, writing for performance, and writing for interactive media.

University of California, Chico
Chico, California
http://www.csuchico.edu/catalog/programs/engl/ma_engl.html
M.A. in English with a creative writing pattern. Two or more years (30 degree hours) in fiction, poetry, or playwriting.

California State University, Fresno
Fresno, California

http://www.csufresno.edu/crwr/
M.F.A., two or more years (54 degree hours), in poetry and fiction.

Humboldt State University
Arcata, California
http://www.humboldt.edu/~english/grad.html
M.A. in English with concentration in teaching of writing. Two years (36 degree hours).

Loyola Marymount University
Los Angeles, California
http://bellarmine.lmu.edu/english/graduate.htm
M.A. in English with creative writing emphasis. Two years.

Mills College
Oakland, California
http://www.mills.edu/academics/graduate/eng/degree_requirements.php
M.F.A., two years, in poetry, fiction, creative nonfiction, or children's literature.

New College of California
San Francisco, California
http://www.newcollege.edu/poetics/index.html
M.A. in poetics, two years (36 degree hours).
Note: The program is heavily involved with community and environmental groups through the Center for Education and Social Action (CESA).

New College of California
San Francisco, California
http://www.newcollege.edu/poetics/index.html
M.F.A. in poetics, three or more years (56 degree hours).
Note: The program is heavily involved with community and environmental groups through the Center for Education and Social Action (CESA).

New College of California
San Francisco, California
http://www.newcollege.edu/writingma/index.cfm
M.A./M.F.A. in writing and consciousness. Three or more years (54 degree hours).
Note: "Students complete the M.A. coursework and creative thesis before undertaking the M.F.A. All courses are held on weekends."

Saint Mary's College of California
Moraga, California
http://www.stmarys-ca.edu/academics/adult_graduate/programs_
by_school/school_of_liberal_arts/programs/mfa/programs.html
M.F.A., two years, in fiction, poetry, or nonfiction.

Note: If you're intimidated by the long Web address, try www.stmarys-ca.edu, and then do a search for creative writing. The program is the first link to appear.

San Diego State University
San Diego, California
http://mfa.sdsu.edu/ink.html
M.F.A., three years (54 degree hours), in fiction or poetry.

San Francisco State University
San Francisco, California
http://www.sfsu.edu/~cwriting/
M.A. in English, creative writing. Two years (30 degree hours), in fiction, poetry, or playwriting.

San Francisco State University
San Francisco, California
http://www.sfsu.edu/~cwriting/
M.F.A., three years (54 degree hours), in fiction, poetry, or playwriting.

University of San Francisco
San Francisco, California
http://artsci.usfca.edu/academics/graduate/writing/overview.html
M.F.A., two years (33 degree hours), in fiction, poetry, and creative nonfiction.
Note: Classes meet in the evenings.

San Jose State University
San Jose, California
http://www2.sjsu.edu/depts/english/MFA/program.html
M.F.A., three years (48 degree hours), in poetry, fiction, creative nonfiction, and scriptwriting.
Note: The program allows students to concentrate in more than one genre.

Stanford University
Stanford, California
http://www.stanford.edu/dept/english/cw/fellowship.html
Stegner Fellowship, two years, in fiction and poetry.
Note: This fellowship is a non-degree program, often thought of as a post-M.F.A. fellowship, though an advanced degree is not required. All students fully funded. Ten fellows accepted each year.

Sonoma State University
Rohnert Park, California
http://www.sonoma.edu/english/ma.html
M.A. in English with emphasis in creative writing. Two years (34 degree hours).

University of Southern California
Los Angeles, California
http://www.usc.edu/dept/LAS/mpw/
M.P.W. (Master of Professional Writing), two years (30 degree hours). "An interdisciplinary graduate writing program that offers classes in non-fiction, fiction, poetry, playwriting, and screen and television writing."
Note: "Classes meet in the late afternoon and evening hours for the convenience of working adults."

University of Southern California
Los Angeles, California
http://www.usc.edu/dept/publications/cat95/cntv/cntv10.html
"The Master of Fine Arts with a track in Screenwriting is granted by the School of Cinema-Television. It is a two-year program which concentrates in writing for narrative film and television."

COLORADO

Colorado State University
Fort Collins, Colorado
http://www.colostate.edu/Depts/English/programs/mfa.htm
M.F.A., two or three years (48 degree hours), in fiction or poetry with electives in creative nonfiction and translation.

University of Colorado, Boulder
Boulder, Colorado
http://www.colorado.edu/English/academic_programs/crw/CWgrad.htm
M.A. in creative writing. Two years (30 degree hours), in fiction, poetry, nonfiction, scriptwriting, and publishing

University of Denver
Denver, Colorado
http://www.du.edu/english/gradcwr.html
M.A. in English with a concentration in creative writing. Two years in open genres: poetry and prose.
Note: "Although the writing program accepts a small number of M.A. students, the large majority of students are in the Ph.D. program."

Naropa University
Boulder, Colorado
http://www.naropa.edu/writingandpoetics/mfawritingprogram.html
M.F.A. in writing and poetics, in poetry, prose, or translation. Two years (49 degree hours).

CONNECTICUT

University of Connecticut
Storrs, Connecticut
http://www.longriver.uconn.edu/grad.htm
M.A. or Ph.D. in literature.
Note: There is no creative writing option or degree. Instead, graduate students "may participate in a creative writing community that serves to supplement their degree programs, and their writing lives."

Southern Connecticut State University
New Haven, Connecticut
http://www.southernct.edu/departments/english/creativewriting.html
M.A. or M.S. (Master of Science) in English with concentrations in creative writing. Two years (33 degree hours). Fiction, poetry, creative nonfiction, and novel writing.

Yale University
New Haven, Connecticut
http://www.yale.edu/drama/academics/playwriting/
M.F.A., three years, in playwriting

DISTRICT OF COLUMBIA

American University
Washington, DC
http://www.american.edu/cas/lit/mfa-lit.htm
M.F.A., two years (48 degree hours), in poetry, fiction, playwriting, and screenwriting.

FLORIDA

University of Central Florida
Orlando, Florida
http://www.english.ucf.edu/grad/cw.html
M.F.A., two years (36 degree hours), in fiction, poetry, or creative nonfiction.

Florida International University (Biscayne Bay Campus)
North Miami, Florida
http://w3.fiu.edu/crwriting/
M.F.A. in fiction, poetry, creative nonfiction, and screenwriting. Three or more years (48 degree hours).

Florida State University
Tallahassee, Florida
http://www.english.fsu.edu/crw/index.html

M.A. in English with concentration in creative writing, two years, in poetry, fiction, drama, and nonfiction.

University of Florida
Gainesville, Florida
http://www.english.ufl.edu/crw
M.F.A., two years (48 degree hours), in fiction and poetry.
Notes: Six to nine students per year in each genre . . . "All students are supported by a fellowship or teaching assistantship."

University of Miami
Coral Gables, Florida
http://www.as.miami.edu/english/mfa.htm
M.F.A., two years (36 degree hours), in fiction, poetry, or screenwriting.
Note: The M.F.A. in screenwriting is available from the School of Communication. http://com.miami.edu/Graduate/MFAMotionPictures Screenwriting.htm

University of South Florida
Tampa, Florida
http://www.cas.usf.edu/english/grad.html
M.A. in English with creative writing track, in fiction, nonfiction, or poetry. Two years.
Note: A graduate certificate in creative writing is also offered.

GEORGIA

Georgia College & State University
Milledgeville, Georgia
http://al.gcsu.edu/cwprogram.htm
M.F.A., two years (42 degree hours), in fiction, poetry, scriptwriting, and creative nonfiction.

Georgia State University
Atlanta, Georgia
http://www2.gsu.edu/~wwweng/creative_writing/graduate/mfa.html
M.F.A., three years (48 degree hours), in poetry and fiction

Georgia State University
Atlanta, Georgia
http://www2.gsu.edu/~wwweng/creative_writing/graduate/ma.html
M.A. in English with creative writing concentration. Two years (27 degree hours), in fiction and poetry.

University of Georgia
Athens, Georgia
http://www.english.uga.edu/~creative/graduate/ma.html
M.A. in English with creative writing thesis. Two years in fiction, poetry, and creative nonfiction.

Kennesaw State University
Kennesaw, Georgia
http://mapw.kennesaw.edu/
M.A. in professional writing, with concentration in creative writing, in fiction, poetry, playwriting, and nonfiction. Two years (36 degree hours). Note: A graduate certificate in creative writing is also available.

HAWAII

University of Hawaii at Manoa
Honolulu, Hawaii
http://www.hawaii.edu/graduatestudies/fields/html/departments/efg/english/english.htm
M.A. in English with concentration in creative writing. Two years (27 degree hours), in poetry, fiction, or nonfiction.

IDAHO

Boise State University
Boise, Idaho
http://www.boisestate.edu/english/mfa/
M.F.A., three years (48 degree hours), in fiction, creative nonfiction, and poetry.

Idaho State University
Pocatello, Idaho
http://www.isu.edu/english/english-MA.html
M.A. in English with creative thesis option in poetry, fiction, or drama. Two years (33 degree hours).

University of Idaho
Moscow, Idaho
http://www.class.uidaho.edu/english/CW/mfaprogram.html
M.F.A., three years (54 degree hours), in fiction, poetry, and creative nonfiction.

ILLINOIS

The School of the Art Institute of Chicago
Chicago, Illinois

http://www.artic.edu/saic/programs/degrees/graduate/mfaw.html
M.F.A., three to four years (60 degree hours), in a variety of concentrations including prose, poetry, film and video, new media, hybrid works, and collaborative projects.

Bradley University
Peoria, Illinois
http://www.bradley.edu/las/eng/eng_graduate.html
M.A. with writing option.

Columbia College Chicago
Chicago, Illinois
http://www.colum.edu/graduate/04-05/gradcrwr.html (Fiction) or
http://www.colum.edu/graduate/04-05/gradpoetry.html (Poetry)
M.F.A. in fiction or poetry. M.A. in teaching of writing. Three to four years.
Note: The fiction and poetry departments seem to be separate at this school.

Illinois State University
Normal, Illinois
http://www.english.ilstu.edu/coursecatalog.htm
M.A. in writing, with concentrations in writing or pedagogy.

University of Illinois at Chicago
Chicago, Illinois
http://www.uic.edu/depts/engl/programs/grad_english/masters/masters_info.htm
M.A. in English with specialization in creative writing, in fiction or poetry. Two years (32 degree hours).
Note: Some specifics are subject to change. The Web site promises "a full-scale curricular revision of the graduate program."

University of Illinois at Urbana Champaign
Urbana, Illinois
http://www.english.uiuc.edu/mfa/index.shtml
M.F.A., three years (48 degree hours), in fiction and poetry.
Note: This site actually lists the e-mail addresses of a half-dozen current students so that prospective students may e-mail them with questions. Impressive.

Northwestern University
Evanston, Illinois
http://www.scs.northwestern.edu/grad/cw/
M.A. in creative writing, in fiction, poetry, or creative nonfiction. Two or more years.
Note: A part-time evening master's program.

Roosevelt University
Chicago, Illinois
http://www.roosevelt.edu/cas/sls/writing.htm
M.F.A., three years (42 degree hours), in fiction, poetry, or creative nonfiction.
Note: The program also offers courses in playwriting, screenwriting, and literary magazine production.

Southern Illinois University at Carbondale
Carbondale, Illinois
http://www.siu.edu/departments/english/GraduateStudies/GradIndex percent20Spring-05.htm
M.F.A. (studio/academic), three years (according to AWP Guide), 48 degree hours, fiction, poetry, or a combination.

Southern Illinois University at Edwardsville
Edwardsville, Illinois
http://www.siue.edu/ENGLISH/CW/index.html
M.A. in English, creative writing specialization, in fiction, creative nonfiction, and poetry. Two years (30 degree hours).

Western Illinois University
Macomb, Illinois
http://www.wiu.edu/english/graduate/
M.A. in English, writing option. Two years (33 degree hours).

INDIANA

Ball State University
Muncie, Indiana
http://www.bsu.edu/shapps/english/cwp/gradcatalog.htm
M.A. in English (creative writing). Two years (33 degree hours).

Indiana State University
Terre Haute, Indiana
http://web.indstate.edu/english/creative.html
M.A. in English with specialization in writing. Two years (32 degree hours).
Note: "Most current graduate students in English, including first-year students, hold assistantships that provide a stipend and a tuition waiver."

Indiana University
Bloomington, Indiana
http://www.indiana.edu/~mfawrite/
M.F.A., three years (60 degree hours), in fiction and poetry.
Note: Twelve graduate students accepted per year. All students funded.

Indiana University
Bloomington, Indiana
http://www.indiana.edu/~mfawrite/
M.A. in creative writing. Two years (30 degree hours), in fiction and poetry.
Note: All students funded.

University of Notre Dame
Notre Dame, Indiana
http://www.nd.edu/~alcwp/
M.F.A., two years, in fiction, poetry, or creative nonfiction.
Note 1: Ten writers admitted per year.
Note 2: All accepted students receive full tuition waivers.

Purdue University, M.F.A.
West Lafayette, Indiana
http://www.sla.purdue.edu/academic/engl/CreativeWriting/index.html
M.F.A., three years (42 degree hours), in fiction and poetry.

IOWA

Iowa State University
Ames, Iowa
http://www.engl.iastate.edu/graduatestudies/CWsite/home.html
M.A. in English with specialization in creative writing. Two years (30 degree hours), in fiction, poetry, and nonfiction.

University of Iowa
Iowa City, Iowa
http://www.uiowa.edu/~iww/ (fiction and poetry)
http://www.english.uiowa.edu/nonfiction/ (nonfiction)
http://www.uiowa.edu/ percent7Etheatre/programs/playwriting.htm (playwriting)
M.F.A., two to three years (48 degree hours), in fiction, poetry, nonfiction, and playwriting.

University of Northern Iowa
Cedar Falls, Iowa
http://www.uni.edu/english/web/GradEnglish.htm
M.A. major in English, creative writing emphasis, in poetry or fiction. Two years (36 degree hours).

KANSAS

Emporia State University
Emporia, Kansas

http://www.emporia.edu/english/graduate.html
M.A. in English with creative writing study.

Kansas State University
Manhattan, Kansas
http://www.ksu.edu/english/programs/graduatestudies.html
M.A. in English with emphasis in creative writing, in fiction, poetry, drama, or nonfiction. Two years (33 degree hours).

University of Kansas
Lawrence, Kansas
http://www.ku.edu/~english/graduate_program.htm
M.A. in English with creative writing and literature option, in fiction, poetry, drama, or nonfiction. Two years.

Wichita State University
Wichita, Kansas
http://webs.wichita.edu/cwfwww/
M.F.A., three years (48 degree hours), in fiction or poetry.

Wichita State University
Wichita, Kansas
http://webs.wichita.edu/?u=english&p=/graduate/maprog
M.A. in English with creative thesis in fiction or poetry. Twenty-four degree hours.

KENTUCKY

University of Louisville
Louisville, Kentucky
http://coldfusion.louisville.edu/webs/a-s/english/grad.cfm?page=masters
M.A. in English with emphasis in creative writing. Two years (30 degree hours).

Morehead State University
Morehead, Kentucky
http://www.moreheadstate.edu/units/Graduate/mae.html
M.A. in English with creative writing emphasis, in poetry, fiction, and creative nonfiction. Two years (33 degree hours).

Murray State University
Murray, Kentucky
http://www.murraystate.edu/chfa/english/MA-Creative.htm
M.A. in English with emphasis in creative writing, in poetry or fiction. Two years (30 degree hours).

LOUISIANA

University of Louisiana at Lafayette
Lafayette, Louisiana
http://english.louisiana.edu/degrees/masters/index.shtml
M.A. in English with creative writing option. Two years (33 degree hours).

Louisiana State University
Baton Rouge, Louisiana
http://english.lsu.edu/dept/programs/creative_writing
M.F.A., three years, in a variety of genres, including fiction, poetry, literary nonfiction, screenwriting, and translation.
Note: Twenty-five to thirty students in the program.

McNeese State University
Lake Charles, Louisiana
http://www.mfa.mcneese.edu/index.htm
M.F.A., three years (60 degree hours), in poetry or fiction.

University of New Orleans
New Orleans, Louisiana
http://www.uno.edu/~cww/
M.F.A. in drama and communications, creative writing. In fiction writing, nonfiction writing, playwriting, poetry and fiction, and screenwriting. Two or more years (45 degree hours).

MAINE

University of Maine, Orono
Orono, Maine
http://www.umaine.edu/english/CW.htm
M.A. in English with concentration in creative writing, in fiction, poetry, or creative nonfiction. Two years (30 degree hours).

MARYLAND

University of Baltimore
Baltimore, Maryland
http://raven.ubalt.edu/programs/mfacreativewriting
M.F.A. in creative writing and publishing arts. Two to three years (48 degree hours), in poetry, fiction, and/or nonfiction.
Note: Fifteen entering students; no more than thirty at a time enrolled.

Johns Hopkins University
Baltimore, Maryland
http://www.jhu.edu/~writsem/gradprogram05.html

M.F.A., two years, in fiction and poetry.
Note: "All students will receive financial aid in the form of full tuition and teaching assistantship."

Johns Hopkins University
Baltimore, Maryland
http://www.jhu.edu/~writsem/gradprogram05.html
M.A. in science writing. One year.

Johns Hopkins University
Baltimore, Maryland
http://www.jhu.edu/pgp-as/writing/
M.A. in writing. This program is intended for part-time students. "Allows students in the Washington-Baltimore region to earn a creative writing degree at their own speed while maintaining full-time jobs or meeting other obligations."

University of Maryland
College Park, Maryland
http://www.english.umd.edu/programs/CreateWriting/index.html
M.F.A., two years (36 degree hours), in fiction or poetry.

Towson University
Towson, Maryland
http://wwwnew.towson.edu/english/PW/prowrinf.htm
M.S. (Master of Science) in professional writing. Two or more years (36 degree hours).
Note: The program enrolls part-time students and is available through evening and summer schedules.

MASSACHUSETTS

Boston University
Boston, Massachusetts
http://www.bu.edu/writing/index.html
M.A. in creative writing in fiction, poetry, or playwriting. One year.
Note: Thirty students accepted each year.

Boston University
Boston, Massachusetts
http://www.bu.edu/com/filmtv/gradscreenwriting.html
M.F.A. in screenwriting.

Emerson College
Boston, Massachusetts
http://www.emerson.edu/writing_lit_publishing/index.cfm?doc_id=184

M.F.A. in poetry, fiction, nonfiction, playwriting, and scriptwriting. Three to five years.
Note: There is also an M.A. in publishing and writing.

Massachusetts Institute of Technology
Cambridge, Massachusetts
http://web.mit.edu/sciwrite/
M.S. in science writing. One year.

University of Massachusetts
Amherst, Massachusetts
http://www.umass.edu/english/eng/mfa/main.html
M.F.A., three to four years (60 degree hours), in fiction or poetry.

University of Massachusetts, Boston
Boston, Massachusetts
http://www.umb.edu/academics/departments/english/undergraduate/
programscert.html
Certificates in creative writing, professional writing, and technical writing.

University of Massachusetts, Dartmouth
North Dartmouth, Massachusetts
http://www.umassd.edu/cas/english/professional_writing/welcomepwp.cfm
M.A. in professional writing, two years, with concentrations in journalism, electronic publishing, technical, business, screen, grant, and creative writing.

Northeastern University
Boston, Massachusetts
http://www.vineyardworkshops.neu.edu/program.html
M.A.W. (Master of Arts in Writing).
Note 1: Northeastern University's M.A. in writing is intended primarily for teachers, elementary through college levels. All courses required for completing the degree are offered at Martha's Vineyard through the Institute on Writing, Reading, and Teaching. The degree may be completed in as few as three to four years, combining intensive summer sessions with writing and research projects conducted during the year.
Note 2: This degree is through Northeastern University. You'll have to piece together information from the above site as well as http://www.casdn. neu.edu/~english/grad/

MICHIGAN

Central Michigan University
Mt. Pleasant, Michigan
http://www.chsbs.cmich.edu/English_Graduate/creative_writ.htm

M.A. in English language and literature with concentration in creative writing. Two years (30 degree hours), in fiction or poetry.

University of Michigan
Ann Arbor, Michigan
http://www.lsa.umich.edu/english/grad/mfa/
M.F.A., two years (36 degree hours), in fiction or poetry.
Note: "In the first year, all M.F.A. students accepted into the program are offered from a 71 percent to a full tuition waiver and corresponding stipend either through a Gradership or by fellowship . . . Second year support includes a complete tuition waiver, stipend, and health care benefits through a Graduate Student Instructorship."

Northern Michigan University
Marquette, Michigan
http://www.nmu.edu/mfa/
M.F.A., three years (48 degree hours), in creative nonfiction, fiction, or poetry.

Wayne State University
Detroit, Michigan
http://www.english.wayne.edu/Concentrations/creative_writing/
M.A. in English with creative writing emphasis, in poetry, fiction, and writing for the theatre. Two years (33 degree hours).
M.A. in English with technical writing emphasis. Two years (33 degree hours).

Western Michigan University
Kalamazoo, Michigan
http://www.wmich.edu/english/grad.html
M.F.A. in fiction, poetry, nonfiction, or playwriting.
Note: This Web site is very poorly designed. Be sure to click on FAQ, Master of Fine Arts, General Information, and Masters Degree Programs, which are spread all over the page and often open in Word format.

MINNESOTA

Hamline College
Saint Paul, Minnesota
http://www.hamline.edu/gls/current_new/mfa_degree_program.html
M.F.A., three years (48 degree hours), in poetry, fiction, creative nonfiction, children's literature, or any combination of genres.
Note: There is also a Master of Liberal Studies Degree (M.A.L.S.), where students may concentrate in creative writing along with other interdisciplinary studies.

Minnesota State University, Mankato
Mankato, Minnesota
http://www.english.mnsu.edu/web/gradCreativeWriting.htm
M.F.A., two to three years (48 degree hours), in poetry and prose.

Minnesota State University, Moorhead
Moorhead, Minnesota
http://www.mnstate.edu/finearts/
M.F.A., three years (42 degree hours), in poetry, fiction, playwriting, screen-writing, or creative nonfiction.

University of Minnesota
Minneapolis, Minnesota
http://english.cla.umn.edu/creativewriting/programinfo/programinfo.html
M.F.A., three years (46 degree hours), in poetry, fiction, or literary nonfiction.
Note: "The English Department at the University of Minnesota is commit-ted to providing financial support to M.F.A. students for three full years."

St. Cloud State University
St. Cloud, Minnesota
http://bulletin.stcloudstate.edu/gb/programs/engl.asp
M.A. in English with creative thesis. Two years (36 degree hours).

University of St. Thomas
Saint Paul, Minnesota
http://www.stthomas.edu/english/
M.A. in English with creative writing aspect.
Note: This Web site was broken at the time of research.

Winona State University
Winona, Minnesota
http://www.winona.edu/english/
M.A. in English with creative writing thesis in "poetry, fiction, creative prose, drama, or (with committee approval) some combination of genres." Two years (30 degree hours).
Note: Not the best-designed site. Go to the English address above, then Graduate, then you'll need to click on some combination of Overview, Thesis Option, and Graduate Catalog to find the relevant information.

MISSISSIPPI

University of Mississippi
Oxford, Mississippi
http://www.olemiss.edu/depts/english/mfa/home.htm
M.F.A., three years (42 degree hours), in fiction and poetry.

Mississippi State University
Mississippi State, Mississippi
http://www.msstate.edu/dept/english/CWHome.html
M.A. in English with an emphasis in creative writing, in poetry or fiction.
Two years (30 degree hours).

University of Southern Mississippi
Hattiesburg, Mississippi
http://usmenglish.com/Graduatepercent20Links/graduate-MA-require-
ments.htm
M.A. in English, creative writing, in fiction or poetry. Two years (30 degree
hours).

MISSOURI

Southwest Missouri State University
Springfield, Missouri
http://www.smsu.edu/English/graduate_degree_programs.htm
M.A. in English, creative writing track. Two years (32 degree hours).

University of Missouri, Columbia
Columbia, Missouri
http://web.missouri.edu/~cwp/
Creative writing M.A. in English, two years (30 degree hours), in fiction,
poetry, or creative nonfiction.
Note: "All students admitted to the graduate program in creative writing
receive either a fellowship or teaching assistantship."

University of Missouri, Kansas City
Kansas City, Missouri
http://iml.umkc.edu/english/programs/pwe.htm
M.A. in English with a creative writing emphasis in fiction or poetry. Two
years (33 degree hours).

University of Missouri, St. Louis
St. Louis, Missouri
www.umsl.edu/divisions/artscience/english/creative/master_of_fine_arts.htm
M.F.A., two years (39 degree hours), in fiction or poetry.
Note: Forty students total in the program.˘

Washington University
St. Louis, Missouri
http://www.artsci.wustl.edu/~english/writing/
M.F.A., two years (39 degree hours), in fiction and poetry.
Note 1: Around ten students enrolled each year.
Note 2: All students fully funded.

MONTANA

University of Montana
Missoula, Montana
http://www.umt.edu/english/creative_writing/default.htm
M.F.A., two years (45 degree hours), in prose and poetry.
Note: Approximately forty-five students total in the program.

University of Montana
Missoula, Montana
http://www.umt.edu/evst/students_grad_emphasis_writing.htm
M.S. in environmental studies with emphasis in environmental writing.
Two years (33 degree hours), in environmental or nature writing, or the writing of place or landscape.

NEBRASKA

Creighton University
Omaha, Nebraska
http://mockingbird.creighton.edu/english/grad11.htm
M.A. in English with creative writing track. Two years (33 degree hours), in poetry, fiction, and creative nonfiction.

University of Nebraska at Kearney
Kearney, Nebraska
http://www.unk.edu/acad/english/courses/creative-writing.html
M.A. in English with creative writing emphasis, in fiction, poetry, creative nonfiction, or drama writing. Two years (30 degree hours).

University of Nebraska, Lincoln
Lincoln, Nebraska
http://www.unl.edu/english/programs/creative.htm
M.A. in English with concentration in creative writing, in poetry and fiction. Two years (30 degree hours).

University of Nevada, Las Vegas
Las Vegas, Nevada
http://www.unlv.edu/Colleges/Liberal_Arts/English/
M.F.A., three years 54 degree hours), in fiction or poetry.
Note 1: "Almost all our students who wish to be are fully supported by Graduate Assistantships in a thriving teacher-training environment."
Note 2: "The UNLV program stresses the importance of an international focus in writing. As such, at least six hours may be taken at an approved program overseas for an International Emphasis. Additionally, the Peace Corps Track allows students to simultaneously serve with the Corps and complete the requirements of the program in two years. "

University of Nevada, Reno
Reno, Nevada
http://www.unr.edu/cla/engl/program/graduate/bulletin/ma-engl.html
M.A. in English with a writing emphasis, in imaginative or expository writing. Two or more years (31 degree hours).

NEW HAMPSHIRE

University of New Hampshire
Durham, New Hampshire
http://www.unh.edu/english/graduate/mawrit.html
M.A. in English with option in writing, in fiction, nonfiction, or poetry. Two years (32 degree hours).
Note: The program is considering the addition of an M.F.A. program.
Note 2: Accepts fifteen to twenty students each year.

NEW JERSEY

Rutgers University
Camden, New Jersey
http://camden-www.rutgers.edu/dept-pages/english/Pages/creative_writing_track.htm
M.A. in English with creative writing track. Two years (30 degree hours).

William Paterson University
Wayne, New Jersey
http://www.wpunj.edu/cohss/english
M.A. in English with concentration in writing. Two or more years (33 degree hours).
Note: "The department enrolls about 70 graduate students. Nearly all students in the graduate program are employed, most of them full time. They are primarily local area high school teachers and administrators, people who work in the New York/New Jersey business sector, recent college graduates who are considering careers as writers and editors, or students who will be applying to schools that grant professional or doctoral degrees."

NEW MEXICO

New Mexico State University
Las Cruces, New Mexico
http://www.nmsu.edu/~english/programs/mfacw.htm
M.F.A. in English with emphasis in creative writing, in fiction or poetry. Three years (54 degree hours).

University of New Mexico
Albuquerque, New Mexico
http://www.unm.edu/~english/GraduateStudies/MA/CreativeWriting.htm
M.A. in creative writing, in poetry, fiction, or nonfiction. Two or more years
(34 degree hours).
Note: Promises an M.F.A. program soon.

NEW YORK

Binghamton University
Binghamton, New York
http://english.binghamton.edu/gradprog/
M.A. in English with a creative writing concentration in fiction or poetry.

Brooklyn College
Brooklyn, New York
http://depthome.brooklyn.cuny.edu/english/graduate/mfa/geninfo.htm
M.F.A., two years, in fiction, poetry, and playwriting.

City College of New York, City University of New York
New York, New York
http://www.ccny.cuny.edu/english/creative_writing.htm
M.A. in English creative writing. Two years (30 degree hours), in fiction,
poetry, or playwriting.

Columbia University
New York, New York
http://arts.columbia.edu/index.cfm?fuseaction=writing_div.main
M.F.A., two years, three for teaching assistants, in fiction, poetry, and
nonfiction.
Note: About seventy students admitted each year.

Cornell University
Ithaca, New York
http://www.arts.cornell.edu/english/grad.html
M.F.A. in creative writing. Two years in fiction and poetry.
Note: Approximately eight students accepted per year . . . All students are
fully funded by assistantships . . . There is also a joint M.F.A./Ph.D. degree.

Hofstra University
Hempstead, New York
http://www.hofstra.edu/Academics/HCLAS/EAS/EAS_Creative_Writin
g.cfm
M.A. in English and creative writing. Two years (30 degree hours), in
poetry, fiction, essay, and playwriting.

Fordham University
New York, New York, and Bronx, New York
http://www.fordham.edu/Academics/Programs_at_Fordham_/English/MA_in_English_with_a_8195.html
M.A. in English with a writing concentration. Two years, in poetry, fiction, memoir, creative nonfiction, or genre writing.
Note: According to the Web site: "Official approval is pending to institute this new concentration fully."

Manhattanville College
Purchase, New York
http://www.mville.edu/graduate/ma-w.htm
M.A. in writing. Two or more years (32 degree hours).
Note: "Courses are scheduled in the evenings, in order to meet the needs of working adults. The program can be completed in two years, though students may work at their own pace."

The New School University
New York, New York
http://www.nsu.newschool.edu/writing/
M.F.A., two years (36 degree hours), in fiction, poetry, nonfiction, and writing for children.

New York University
New York, New York
http://cwp.fas.nyu.edu/page/grad_programs
M.A. in English with a focus in creative writing, two years (32 degree hours), in fiction or poetry.

New York University
New York, New York
http://cwp.fas.nyu.edu/page/grad_programs
M.F.A., two years (32 degree hours), in fiction or poetry.

Queens College, City University of New York
Flushing, New York
http://qcpages.qc.edu/ENGLISH/Graduate/writingma.html
M.A. in creative writing, two or more years (30 degree hours).
Note 1: Classes are held in the evenings.
Note 2: This Web site will not win the "best designed" or "most informative" contests.

Sarah Lawrence College
Bronxville, New York
http://www.slc.edu/grad_writing
M.F.A.

Note: "Students choose to concentrate in fiction, creative nonfiction, or poetry, but they may take craft courses in genres other than their concentration. Students may study either on a full- or part-time basis."

State University of New York, Albany
Albany, New York
http://www.albany.edu/english/m__a__program.htm
M.A. in English with emphasis in creative writing, in poetry, fiction, or creative nonfiction. Two years (32 degree hours).

State University of New York at Brockport
Brockport, New York
http://www.brockport.edu/english/
M.A. in English with creative writing track. Two years.

Syracuse University
Syracuse, New York
http://english.syr.edu/cwp/cwindex.htm
M.F.A., three years (48 degree hours), in poetry or fiction.
Note: The program offers "particularly strong support in the form of fellowships, scholarships, and teaching assistantships to cover the three years of residency."

NORTH CAROLINA

East Carolina University
Greenville, North Carolina
http://www.ecu.edu/english/cw/
M.A. in English with concentration in creative writing. Two years (30 degree hours), in poetry, fiction, creative nonfiction, and scriptwriting.

North Carolina State University
Raleigh, North Carolina
http://www.chass.ncsu.edu/english/englishnew/subpages/graduate/dpgrmf.htm
M.F.A., two years (36 degree hours), in fiction or poetry.

North Carolina State University
Raleigh, North Carolina
http://www.chass.ncsu.edu/english/maprog/mma.html
M.A. in English with a concentration in creative writing, two years (31 degree hours), in fiction, poetry, or screenwriting.

University of North Carolina at Greensboro
Greensboro, North Carolina
http://www.uncg.edu/eng/mfa/

M.F.A., two years (36 degree hours), in fiction or poetry.
Note: Ten to twelve students admitted each fall.

University of North Carolina at Wilmington
Wilmington, North Carolina
http://www.uncw.edu/writers/mfa-about.html
M.F.A., three years (48 degree hours), in fiction, poetry, creative nonfiction
Note: Fifteen to twenty writers admitted annually

Western Carolina University
Cullowhee, North Carolina
http://www.wcu.edu/as/english
M.A. in English with creative writing thesis. Two years (30 degree hours).

NORTH DAKOTA

University of North Dakota
Grand Forks, North Dakota
http://www.und.edu/dept/english/GradInfo.html
M.A. in English with creative thesis option.

OHIO

Bowling Green State University
Bowling Green, Ohio
http://www.bgsu.edu/departments/creative-writing/home.html
M.F.A., two years (40 degree hours), in poetry and fiction.

University of Cincinnati
Cincinnati, Ohio
http://asweb.artsci.uc.edu/english/Graduate/gradma.htm
M.A. in English with options in creative writing (fiction or poetry), professional writing, or editing and publishing.

Cleveland State University
Cleveland, Ohio
http://www.csuohio.edu/gradcollege/gradbulletin/section02/english.html
M.A. in English with creative writing concentration. Two years (33 degree hours), in fiction, poetry, or playwriting.
Note: Admission to the creative writing concentration is a separate decision made by the creative writing faculty once a student has been admitted into the M.A. program.

John Carroll University
University Heights, Ohio
http://www.jcu.edu/graduate/bulletin/bulletin2004/academic/english.html
M.A. in English with creative writing thesis. Two years (30 degree hours).
Note: This Web site is from the graduate bulletin. The English department
site was under construction.

Miami University
Oxford, Ohio
http://www.units.muohio.edu/english/gradcw/index.html
M.A. in creative writing, two years, in poetry, fiction, or creative nonfiction.
Note: "Almost all students admitted to the M.A. program in creative writ-
ing hold generous Graduate Assistantships."

Ohio State University
Columbus, Ohio
http://english.osu.edu/areas/creative_writing/
M.F.A., three years (70 degree hours), in poetry, creative nonfiction, or fiction.

Ohio University
Athens, Ohio
http://www.english.ohiou.edu/grad/area/cw/
M.A. in creative writing, two years, in poetry, fiction, or nonfiction.

Wright State University
Dayton, Ohio
http://www.cola.wright.edu/Dept/ENG/grlit.htm
M.A. in English with creative writing option. Two years (48 degree hours).
Note: Click on "Elective Options" for creative writing information.

OKLAHOMA

University of Central Oklahoma
Edmond, Oklahoma
*The Web site for this program seems to have disappeared. The school's Web site is
http://www.ucok.edu/ and a very bare English department page can be found at
http://www.libarts.ucok.edu/english/*
M.A. in English with creative writing emphasis.
Note: The status of this program is unknown. E-mail correspondence was
not returned.

Oklahoma State University
Stillwater, Oklahoma
http://english.okstate.edu/grad/index.htm
M.A. in English, two years (30 degree hours).

Note: The OSU program allows for flexibility in combining student interests. Options include: literature, creative writing, film, composition, technical writing, linguistics, and teaching English as a second language.

OREGON

Oregon State University
Corvallis, Oregon
http://oregonstate.edu/dept/english/crw/
M.F.A., two years (48 degree hours), in fiction.
Note 1: The program plans to add a poetry component in the near future.
Note 2: There is also a Master of Arts in Interdisciplinary Study, which includes creative writing as one of four concentrations.

University of Oregon
Eugene, Oregon
http://darkwing.uoregon.edu/~crwrweb/
M.F.A., two years (72 degree hours), in fiction or poetry.
Note: The 72 degree hours is reflective of additional hour credit for workshops and thesis. Students take between two and three classes a quarter.

Portland State University
Portland, Oregon
http://www.english.pdx.edu/grad_wr.html
M.A. in writing *and* M.S. (Master of Science) in writing. Three years (48 degree hours).
Note: Concentrations in creative, nonfiction, professional and technical writing, and book publishing.

PENNSYLVANIA

Arcadia University
Glenside, Pennsylvania
http://www.arcadia.edu/academic/default.aspx?pid=561
M.A. in English with writing emphasis. Two years (36 degree hours).

Bucknell University
Lewisburg, Pennsylvania
http://www.bucknell.edu/Academics/Graduate_Studies/College_of_Arts_and_Sciences/English.html
M.A. in English with creative writing emphasis. Two years.

Pennsylvania State University
University Park, Pennsylvania
http://english.la.psu.edu/area.asp?id=9&
M.F.A., three year (42 degree hours), in fiction, creative nonfiction, poetry.

University of Pittsburgh
Pittsburgh, Pennsylvania
http://www.english.pitt.edu/graduate/mfa.html
M.F.A., three years (36 degree hours), in fiction, poetry, or creative nonfiction.

Temple University
Philadelphia, Pennsylvania
http://www.temple.edu/CreativeWriting/
M.A. in English/creative writing, in poetry and fiction. Two years (30 degree hours).

West Chester University
West Chester, Pennsylvania
http://www.wcupa.edu/_academics/sch_cas.eng/gradprog.htm
M.A. in English with concentration in creative writing, in poetry and fiction. Two years (36 degree hours).

RHODE ISLAND

Brown University
Providence, Rhode Island
http://www.brown.edu/Departments/Literary_Arts/index.html
M.F.A. in literary arts, two years, in fiction, poetry, playwriting, and electronic writing.
Notes: Five fiction writers, five poets, three playwrights, one electronic writer accepted . . . "It is the goal of the Graduate Program in Literary Arts to provide financial aid to all accepted students each year."

Rhode Island College
Providence, Rhode Island
http://www.ric.edu/academics/grad_fas_engcw.html
M.A. in English with concentration in creative writing, in poetry, fiction, nonfictional prose, or drama. Two years (30 degree hours).

SOUTH CAROLINA

University of South Carolina
Colombia, South Carolina
http://www.cas.sc.edu/engl/grad/mfa.html
M.F.A., three years (45 degree hours), in poetry and fiction.

SOUTH DAKOTA

University of South Dakota
Vermillion, South Dakota

http://www.usd.edu/engl/madegree.cfm
M.A. in English with creative writing track. Two years (30 degree hours).

TENNESSEE

Austin Peay State University
Clarksville, Tennessee
http://www.apsu.edu/langlit/graduate.HTM
Creative writing English M.A. One or more years (33 degree hours).

The University of Memphis
Memphis, Tennessee
http://www.people.memphis.edu/ percent7Eegoffice/creative.html
M.A. in creative writing, two years (33 degree hours), in poetry, fiction, or creative nonfiction.

The University of Memphis
Memphis, Tennessee
http://www.people.memphis.edu/ percent7Eegoffice/prowriting.html
M.A. in professional writing. Two years (33 degree hours).

The University of Memphis
Memphis, Tennessee
http://www.people.memphis.edu/ percent7Eegoffice/mfa.html
M.F.A., two or more years (48 degree hours), in poetry, fiction, or creative nonfiction.

University of Tennessee at Chattanooga
Chattanooga, Tennessee
http://www.utc.edu/Academic/English/gprog.html
M.A. in English: writing, in technical writing, creative writing, and professional writing in journalism, public relations, and business. Two years (33 degree hours).

University of Tennessee, Knoxville
Knoxville, Tennessee
http://web.utk.edu/~english/gs_ma_writing.php
M.A. in English with concentration in writing, professional and creative. Two years (24 degree hours).
Note: Funding, in the form of teaching assistantships, is strong here, though the standard teaching load is two classes a semester.

TEXAS

Abilene Christian University
Abilene, Texas

http://www.acu.edu/academics/cas/english/gradprogram/programtracks/writing.html
M.A. in English, with a writing track. Two years (36 degree hours), in fiction, poetry, creative nonfiction, playwriting, composition, or professional writing.

Baylor University
Waco, Texas
http://www.baylor.edu/english/
M.A. in English with creative writing thesis. Two years (30 degree hours).
Note: Ten to fifteen students admitted each year.

Hardin-Simmons College
Abilene, Texas
http://www.hsutx.edu/academics/english/creative_writing/program.html
M.A. in English with creative writing emphasis. Two years (33 degree hours), in poetry and fiction.

University of Houston
Houston, Texas
http://www.class.uh.edu/cwp/
M.F.A., in poetry or fiction. Two years (42 degree hours).
Note 1: Ten poetry, ten fiction students accepted each year.
Note 2 : "Our [Web] site will be going through a major re-design."

University of North Texas
Denton, Texas
http://www.engl.unt.edu/grad/grad_MAcreative.htm
M.A. in creative writing, two years (36 degree hours), in fiction, poetry, creative nonfiction, or screenwriting.

Sam Houston State University
Huntsville, Texas
http://www.shsu.edu/~eng_www/GradProgram/create.html
M.A. in English with creative writing emphasis, two years (36 degree hours).

Southern Methodist University
Dallas, Texas
http://faculty.smu.edu/sshepher/gradbroc.htm
M.A. in English literature and creative writing, in fiction or poetry. Two years (30 degree hours).

Texas A&M University
College Station, Texas
http://www-english.tamu.edu/cw/graduate.html

M.A. in English with creative writing specialization, in fiction, nonfiction, and poetry. Two years (30 degree hours).
Note: Funding is very good here, in the form of teaching and program assistantships.

Texas State University
Sam Marcos, Texas
http://mfa.english.txstate.edu/
M.F.A., three years (48 degree hours), in fiction and poetry.
Note: Ninety percent of students are funded.

Texas Tech University
Lubbock, Texas
http://www.english.ttu.edu/department/read.asp?keyword=me_areas
M.A. in English, with emphasis in creative writing, in fiction, nonfiction, and poetry. Two years (36 degree hours).

University of Texas at Austin (aka the James A. Michener Center for Writers)
Austin, Texas
http://www.utexas.edu/academic/mcw/
M.F.A., three years (54 degree hours), in fiction, poetry, screenwriting, and playwriting (students focus on at least two).
Note: This is the best funding in the country, with each student receiving full tuition waiver and stipend.

University of Texas at Austin
Austin, Texas
http://www.utexas.edu/cola/depts/english/programs/creativewriting/
M.A. in creative writing, in fiction and poetry. Two years (33 degree hours).

University of Texas at Dallas
Richardson, Texas
http://www.utdallas.edu/~nelsen/creativity.html
M.A. with emphasis in creative writing, in fiction, poetry, biography, drama, and translation. Two years (30 degree hours).

University of Texas, El Paso
El Paso, Texas
http://www.utep.edu/cw/
Bilingual M.F.A., in English and Spanish poetry, fiction, creative nonfiction, translation, screenwriting, or playwriting. Three years (48 degree hours).

UTAH

Brigham Young University
Provo, Utah

http://english.byu.edu/emphasis/creative percent20writing/gspage.htm
M.A. in English with creative writing emphasis.

University of Utah
Salt Lake City, Utah
http://www.english.utah.edu/graduate_studies/index.html
M.F.A., two years (33 degree hours), in fiction and poetry.

VERMONT
None

VIRGINIA

George Mason University
Fairfax, Virginia
http://creativewriting.gmu.edu/
M.F.A., three years, in poetry, fiction, and creative nonfiction.

George Mason University
Fairfax, Virginia
http://english.gmu.edu/graduate/ma.html
M.A. in English with concentration in professional writing and editing.
M.A. in English with concentration in teaching of writing and literature.
Certificate: professional writing and editing.
The M.A.s are two years (30 degree hours). The certificate is 18 degree hours.

Hollins University
Roanoke, Virginia
http://www.hollins.edu/grad/eng_writing/eng_writing.htm
M.F.A., two or more years (48 degree hours), in poetry, creative nonfiction,
plays, novels, short fiction, and children's literature.
Note: Twelve students accepted each year.

Hollins University
Roanoke, Virginia
http://www.hollins.edu/grad/childlit/childlit.htm
M.A. and M.F.A. in children's literature.
Note: These are summer-only programs that last from three to five summers.

James Madison University
Harrisonburg, Virginia
http://www.jmu.edu/english/dept/grad.html
M.A. in English with creative writing thesis. Two years (33 degree hours),
in fiction or poetry, with some flexibility for other genres.

Old Dominion University
Norfolk, Virginia
http://al.odu.edu/mfacw/
M.F.A., three years (54 degree hours), in nonfiction, dramatic writing, poetry, and fiction.

University of Virginia
Charlottesville, Virginia
http://www.engl.virginia.edu/cwp/
M.F.A., two years (24 degree hours), in fiction and poetry.
Note 1: Admits seven fiction writers and five poets each year.
Note 2: All students fully funded with writing and teaching fellowships.

Virginia Commonwealth University
Richmond, Virginia
http://www.has.vcu.edu/eng/graduate/mfa.htm
M.F.A., three years (48 degree hours), in fiction and poetry
Note: Courses are "available that focus on writing drama, nonfiction, and screenplays, as well as courses that provide practical experience in editing."

Virginia Tech University
Blacksburg, Virginia
http://www.english.vt.edu/cw/mfa/
M.F.A., three years (48 degree hours), in fiction, poetry, and playwriting.

WASHINGTON STATE

Eastern Washington University
(aka the Inland Northwest Center for Writers)
Spokane, Washington
http://www.ewu.edu/x623.xml
M.F.A. in poetry, fiction and creative nonfiction. Students may attend part-time. Three to six years (72 degree hours).

Western Washington University
Bellingham, Washington
http://www.ac.wwu.edu/~enggrad/
M.A. in English with concentration in writing, in poetry, fiction, and non-fiction. Two years (45 degree hours).

WEST VIRGINIA

West Virginia University
Morgantown, West Virginia
http://www.as.wvu.edu/english/grad/masters.html
M.A. in English, emphasis in creative writing.

West Virginia University
Morgantown, West Virginia
http://www.as.wvu.edu/english/cw/mfa.html
M.F.A., two or more years, in fiction, nonfiction, or poetry.
Note: "Most students admitted into the M.F.A. program receive Graduate Teaching Assistantships that include a stipend [this year $6,264] plus a tuition waiver."

WISCONSIN

University of Wisconsin, Madison
Madison, Wisconsin
http://creativewriting.wisc.edu
M.F.A., two years, in fiction and poetry.
Note 1: "All students will receive two-year teaching assistantships that include annual stipends."
Note 2: Twelve students total.
Note 3: Students in different genres apply in different years (odd/even). Consult the Web site for more information.

University of Wisconsin, Madison
Madison, Wisconsin
http://www.wisc.edu/english/cw/
M.A. in English with creative writing component. Fiction, nonfiction, and poetry.
Note: Look under "Creative Writing for Literary Studies Students" on the creative writing Web page.

University of Wisconsin, Madison
Madison, Wisconsin
http://creativewriting.wisc.edu
Six Writer-in-Resident Fellowships are also available for selected post-M.F.A. or Ph.D. students from any program. One year, in poetry and fiction.

University of Wisconsin, Milwaukee
Milwaukee, Wisconsin
http://www.uwm.edu/Dept/English/cw/index.html
M.A. in English with creative writing emphasis, in poetry and fiction. One or more years (24 degree hours).

WYOMING

University of Wyoming
Laramie, Wyoming
http://uwacadweb.uwyo.edu/creativewriting/
M.F.A., two years (40 degree hours), in poetry, fiction, and creative nonfiction.

University of Wyoming
Laramie, Wyoming
http://uwacadweb.uwyo.edu/english/graduate/graduate_sub.asp
M.A. in English with concentration in creative writing. Two years (30 degree hours).

PH.D. WRITING PROGRAMS IN THE UNITED STATES

Since there are relatively few Ph.D. programs with creative writing aspects (at least compared to M.A. and M.F.A. programs), I've listed these by region instead of state.

NORTHEAST

Binghamton University
Binghamton, New York
http://english.binghamton.edu/gradprog/
Ph.D. in English with creative dissertation in fiction or poetry.

Cornell University
Ithaca, New York
http://www.arts.cornell.edu/english/phd.html
M.F.A./Ph.D. program in English and creative writing.
Note: This is a joint degree program offered to only one or two students per year. The Ph.D. dissertation is not in creative writing.

State University of New York, Albany
Albany, New York
http://www.albany.edu/english/ph__d__program.htm
Ph.D. in English with creative dissertation, in poetry, fiction, or creative nonfiction.

SOUTHEAST

Florida State University
Tallahassee, Florida
http://www.english.fsu.edu/crw/index.html
Ph.D. in English with creative dissertation, in poetry, fiction, drama, and nonfiction.

Georgia State University
Atlanta, Georgia
http://www2.gsu.edu/~wwweng/creative_writing/graduate/phd.html
Ph.D. in creative writing in fiction and poetry.

University of Georgia
Athens, Georgia
http://www.english.uga.edu/~creative/graduate/phd.html
Ph.D. in English with creative writing dissertation, in fiction, poetry, and
creative nonfiction.

University of Louisiana at Lafayette
Lafayette, Louisiana
http://english.louisiana.edu/degrees/masters/index.shtml
Ph.D. in English with creative writing concentration.

University of Southern Mississippi
Hattiesburg, Mississippi
http://usmenglish.com/Graduate percent20Links/graduate-PhD-require-
ments.htm
Ph.D. in English, area of study in creative writing, in fiction or poetry.

University of Tennessee, Knoxville
Knoxville, Tennessee
http://web.utk.edu/~english/gs_phd_creative.php
Ph.D. in English with creative thesis.
Note: Funding, in the form of teaching assistantships, is strong here,
though the standard teaching load is two classes a semester.

MIDWEST

Ball State University
Muncie, Indiana
http://www.bsu.edu/shapps/english/cwp/gradcatalog.htm
Doctoral cognate in creative writing. 15 degree hours.

University of Cincinnati
Cincinnati, Ohio
http://asweb.artsci.uc.edu/english/Graduate/gradphd.htm
Ph.D. in English with a creative dissertation option.

Illinois State University
Normal, Illinois
http://www.english.ilstu.edu/graduate/phdengstudies.htm
Ph.D. in English with creative dissertation.

University of Illinois, Chicago
Chicago, Illinois
http://www.uic.edu/depts/engl/programs/grad_english/grad_english.htm
Ph.D. in English with creative writing specialization.

University of Missouri Columbia
Columbia, Missouri
http://www.missouri.edu/~cwp/
Creative writing Ph.D. in English. Fiction, poetry, or creative nonfiction.
Note: "All students admitted to the graduate program in creative writing receive either a fellowship or teaching assistantship."

University of Nebraska
Lincoln, Nebraska
http://www.unl.edu/english/graduate/grad_PhDdegrees.html
Ph.D. in creative writing
Note: Funding seems very good here, in the form of teaching assistantships.

University of North Dakota
Grand Forks, North Dakota
http://www.und.edu/dept/english/GradInfo.html
Ph.D. in English with creative thesis option.

Ohio University
Athens, Ohio
http://www.english.ohiou.edu/grad/area/cw/
Ph.D. in creative writing, in poetry, fiction, or nonfiction.

Oklahoma State University
Stillwater, Oklahoma
http://english.okstate.edu/grad/index.htm
Ph.D. in English.
Note: The OSU program allows for flexibility in combining student interests. Options include: literature, creative writing, film, composition, technical writing, linguistics, and teaching English as a second language.

University of South Dakota
Vermillion, South Dakota
http://www.usd.edu/engl/phddegree.cfm
Ph.D. in English with creative writing emphasis.

Western Michigan University
Kalamazoo, Michigan
http://www.wmich.edu/english/gradhandbook/index.htm#doctoral
Ph.D. in English with creative writing emphasis, in fiction, nonfiction, poetry, and playwriting.

University of Wisconsin, Madison
Madison, Wisconsin
http://www.wisc.edu/english/cw/
Ph.D. in English with minor in creative writing. Fiction, nonfiction, and poetry.

Note: Look under "Creative Writing for Literary Studies Students" on the creative writing Web page.

University of Wisconsin, Milwaukee
Milwaukee, Wisconsin
http://www.uwm.edu/Dept/English/cw/index.html
Ph.D. in English with creative writing emphasis, in poetry and fiction.
M.A. in English with creative writing emphasis, in poetry and fiction. One or more years (24 degree hours).

SOUTHWEST

University of Houston
Houston, Texas
http://www.class.uh.edu/cwp/
Ph.D. in literature and creative writing, in fiction or poetry.
Note: "Our [Web] site will be going through a major re-design."

University of North Texas
Denton, Texas
http://www.engl.unt.edu/grad/grad_PhDdegreedesc.htm#PhD_requirements
Ph.D. in English, with focus in creative writing.

Texas Tech University
Lubbock, Texas
http://www.english.ttu.edu/cw/phd.htm
Ph.D. in English, with concentration in creative writing, in fiction, nonfiction, and poetry.

University of Texas at Dallas
Richardson, Texas
http://www.utdallas.edu/~nelsen/creativity.html
Ph.D. in writing and translation with creative thesis, in fiction, poetry, nonfiction, drama, screenwriting, and translation.

WEST

University of Denver
Denver, Colorado
http://www.du.edu/english/gradcwr.html
PhD in English with a concentration in creative writing, in open genres: poetry and prose.

University of Hawaii at Manoa
Honolulu, Hawaii

http://www.hawaii.edu/graduatestudies/fields/html/departments/efg/english/
english.htm
Ph.D. in English with concentration in creative writing, in poetry, fiction,
or nonfiction.

University of Nevada, Las Vegas
Las Vegas, Nevada
http://www.unlv.edu/Colleges/Liberal_Arts/English/
Ph.D. in literature with creative dissertation. In fiction or poetry.

University of Southern California
Los Angeles, California
http://www.usc.edu/dept/LAS/english/creative_writing/
Ph.D. in literature and creative writing. Fiction or poetry.

University of Utah
Salt Lake City, Utah
http://www.english.utah.edu/graduate_studies/phd_creative_writing.html
Ph.D. in literature with creative writing emphasis. Fiction and poetry.

LOW-RESIDENCY M.F.A. PROGRAMS

I've decided against organizing low-residency programs by region. While
most programs will require one to two multiple-day residencies on campus,
the real point of taking a low-residency program is of course to allow the
student to stay where he or she currently resides (or intends to travel to).
Please also note: The length of low-residency programs (my notations such
as "two or more years," etc.) varies, as each program allows for some form
of flexibility in completing the degree over a longer term.

Antioch University
Los Angeles, California
http://www.antiochla.edu/programs_mfa.shtml
M.F.A., two to three years in poetry, fiction, and nonfiction (a dual concentration is available).

Antioch College, McGregor
Yellow Springs, Ohio
http://www.mcgregor.edu/ilps/cw/index.html
M.F.A. in fiction, poetry, nonfiction, playwriting, or screenwriting.

Bennington College
Bennington, Vermont
http://www.bennington.edu/graduate/low_residency/menu.htm
M.F.A., two years, in poetry, fiction, or nonfiction.

British Columbia
Vancouver, British Columbia, Canada
http://www.creativewriting.ubc.ca/programs/lowres.cfm
M.F.A., two or more years, fiction, poetry, or nonfiction.

Carlow College
Pittsburgh, Pennsylvania, and Carlow, Ireland
http://gradstudies.carlow.edu/mfa_writing.html
M.F.A., two and a half years (36 degree hours), in fiction, poetry, or creative nonfiction.

University of Denver
Denver, Colorado
http://www.universitycollege.du.edu/program/academic/oncampus/gis/degreeplansoverview.asp?DegreePlanID=42
A Certificate of Advanced Study in fiction, poetry, or nonfiction.

Fairleigh Dickinson
Madison, New Jersey
http://alpha.fdu.edu/becton/writeMFA/overview.html
M.F.A., two or more years, in fiction, poetry, or creative nonfiction.

Goddard College
Plainfield, Vermont
http://www.goddard.edu/academic/MFAcreativewriting.html
M.F.A., two or more years (48 degree hours), in poetry, fiction, creative nonfiction, memoir, playwriting, screenwriting, or cross genre.

Goucher College
Baltimore, Maryland
http://www.goucher.edu/mfa/index.cfm
M.F.A., two or more years (36 degree hours), in creative nonfiction.

Lancaster University
Lancaster, United Kingdom
http://www.lancs.ac.uk/depts/cw/ma1dist.htm
M.A. in creative writing. Distance learning.
Note: This is not your average graduate program. You'll have to visit the site to see what I mean. Definitely interesting.

Lesley University
Cambridge, Massachusetts
http://www.lesley.edu/gsass/creative_writing/
M.F.A., two years, in poetry, creative nonfiction, fiction, and children's literature.

Murray State University
Murray, Kentucky
http://www.murraystate.edu/chfa/english/mfa/
M.F.A., two years or more years (48 degree hours), in poetry, fiction, and creative nonfiction.

Naropa University
Boulder, Colorado
http://www.naropa.edu/mfaonline/
M.F.A., three years (49 degree hours), in creative writing (no concentration).

University of Nebraska
Omaha, Nebraska
http://avalon.unomaha.edu/unmfaw/
M.F.A., two or more years (60 degree hours), in fiction, poetry, or nonfiction.

New England College
Henniker, New Hampshire
http://www.nec.edu/graduate/mfa/mfa.html
M.F.A., three years (64 degree hours), in poetry.

New Orleans University
New Orleans, Louisiana
http://lowres.uno.edu/lowres.htm
M.F.A., two to four years (45 degree hours), in fiction, poetry, screenwriting, and playwriting.
Other: Has an interesting study-abroad program in Spain, France, and Italy.

Pacific University (aka Mountain Writers Series)
Forest Grove, Oregon
http://www.pacificu.edu/as/mfa/index.cfm
M.F.A., two to three years, in fiction, poetry, and creative nonfiction.

Pacific Lutheran University (aka The Rainier Writing Workshop)
Tacoma, Washington
http://www.plu.edu/~mfa/
M.F.A., three years, in fiction, poetry, and nonfiction.

Queens University of Charlotte
Charlotte, North Carolina
http://www.queens.edu/graduate/programs/creative_writing.asp
M.F.A., two years, in fiction, poetry, and creative nonfiction.

Seattle Pacific University
Seattle, Washington
http://www.spu.edu/prospects/grad/academics/mfa/index.asp

M.F.A., three or more years (64 degree hours), in fiction, poetry, and creative nonfiction.
Other: The program seeks writers who wish to "place their work within the larger context of the Judeo-Christian tradition of faith."

Seton Hill
Greensburg, Pennsylvania
http://www.setonhill.edu/academics/wpf_homepage.cfm?ACID=102
M.A. in writing popular fiction, two years (36 degree hours), with concentrations in mystery, romance, science fiction, horror, fantasy, and children and adolescent fiction.

University of Southern Maine (aka Stonecoast)
Portland, Maine
http://www.usm.maine.edu/stonecoastmfa/
M.F.A., two years (60 degree hours), in poetry, fiction, creative nonfiction, and popular fiction.

Spalding University
Louisville, Kentucky
http://www.spalding.edu/mfa
M.F.A., two or more years (64 degree hours), in fiction, poetry, creative nonfiction, writing for children, and playwriting/screenwriting.

Vermont College
Montpelier, Vermont
http://www.tui.edu/prospective/ma/default.asp?strLink=K.2.2.3
M.F.A. in writing, two years (64 degree hours), in fiction, poetry, and creative nonfiction.
M.F.A. in children's fiction, two years (64 degree hours).

Warnborough University, United Kingdom
Warnborough University is incorporated in the Republic of Ireland as an independent global university for on-site and distance learning.
http://www.warnborough.edu/faculties/arts/mcreative.htm
M.A. in creative writing, two years (40 degree hours), in poetry, fiction, creative nonfiction, or playwriting.
M.F.A., two or more years (80 degree hours), in poetry, fiction, creative nonfiction, or playwriting.
Ph.D. in creative writing, in poetry, fiction, creative nonfiction, or playwriting.
Note 1: Students may study in more than one genre.
Note 2: The program is distance learning, rather than low residency.

Warren Wilson College
Asheville, North Carolina

http://www.warren-wilson.edu/~mfa/
M.F.A., two years, in fiction and poetry.

Western Connecticut State University
Danbury, Connecticut
https://www.wcsu.edu/english/mfa/
M.F.A. in professional writing. Two years.
Note: The program offers study in multiple genres.

Whidbey Writers Workshop
Whidbey Island, Washington
http://www.writeonwhidbey.org/mfa/index.htm
M.F.A., children's literature, creative nonfiction, fiction, and poetry.
Note: "Students may work at their own pace, taking from two to six years
to complete the program."

Wilkes University
Wilkes-Barre, Pennsylvania
http://www.wilkes.edu/creativewriting/default.asp
M.F.A., two years (30 degree hour), in fiction, poetry, screenwriting, playwriting, and creative nonfiction.

GRADUATE WRITING PROGRAMS
OUTSIDE THE UNITED STATES

Note: I've tracked down as many of these as I could. There is not a defini-
tive source; in fact, I'm afraid *this* list will now be the closest to a definitive
source. That said, the best site on the Web for information about writing
programs outside the United States is "Creative Writing Graduate Programs
Outside U.S.A.," where there is basic information plus lists of e-mail contacts.
The address is http://www.gradschools.com/listings/out/creative_write_out.html
There are also a few low-residency writing programs based outside the
United States, but I have listed these in the low-residency section.

Master's Programs

AUSTRALIA and NEW ZEALAND

Macquarie University
Sydney Australia
http://www.international.mq.edu.au/study/postgraduate/areas_coursede-
tails.asp?cse=68
M.A. in creative writing.

University of Adelaide
Adelaide, Australia
http://www.arts.adelaide.edu.au/humanities/english/creative/pg.html
M.A. in creative writing.

University of Melbourne
Melbourne, Australia
http://www.sca.unimelb.edu.au/cw/MCW.html
Master's of creative writing.

University of New South Wales
Sydney, Australia
http://english.arts.unsw.edu.au/engl/pgresearch_current/cwresdegrees.html
M.A. in creative writing.

Victoria University of Wellington
Wellington, New Zealand
http://www.vuw.ac.nz/modernletters/creative-writing/postgraduate.aspx
M.A. in creative writing.

CANADA

University of Alberta, Edmonton
Edmonton, Alberta, Canada
http://www.humanities.ualberta.ca/english/maprogram.html
M.A. in English with creative thesis. One to two years.

University of British Columbia
Vancouver, British Columbia, Canada
http://www.creativewriting.ubc.ca/
M.F.A., two years, in fiction, poetry, nonfiction, writing for children, translation, stage play, radio, screenwriting, or song lyric and libretto.

University of Calgary
Calgary, Alberta, Canada
http://www.english.ucalgary.ca/creative/
M.A. in English with creative writing option, two years, in fiction and/or poetry.
Note: There is a strongly worded statement on the Web site that indicates that very few students are allowed to pursue a creative writing project.

Concordia University
Montreal, Quebec, Canada
http://artsandscience.concordia.ca/English/Program_Information.html
M.A. in English with creative writing option. Two or more years in fiction, poetry, and playwriting.

University of New Brunswick
Fredericton, New Brunswick, Canada
http://www.unbf.ca/english/graduate/gradma.htm
M.A. in English with a concentration in creative writing, in poetry, drama, fiction, or nonfiction. Two years (24 degree hours).

University of Windsor
Windsor, Ontario, Canada
http://www.uwindsor.ca/english
M.A. in English literature and creative writing
Note: The Web address for the creative writing option is three lines long. So, navigate to the above address and then take the path (on the left) Programs in English→ Graduate Studies.

IRELAND

Trinity College
Dublin, Ireland
http://www.tcd.ie/OWC/courses/creative/index.html
M.Phil. in creative writing. One year, in fiction or poetry.

REPUBLIC OF KOREA

Chung-Ang University
Ansung-Kun, Kyungki-Do, Republic of Korea
http://dic.cau.ac.kr/index_e.html
M.A. in creative literature.
Note: There was no available Web page for the creative writing program.

MEXICO

Universidad Intercontinental
Tlalpan, Mexico
http://www.uic.edu.mx/
Master's in scriptwriting.

THE PHILIPPINES

De La Salle University
Manila, Philippines
http://www.dlsu.edu.ph/research/centers/bnscwc/default.asp
M.A. in creative writing.

University of Santo Tomas
Manila, Philippines
http://webservice.mnl.ust.edu.ph/gradsch/courses.htm

M.A. in creative writing.
Note: A prospectus can be downloaded near the bottom of this general page.

SPAIN

Escuela TAI
Madrid, Spain
http://www.escuela-tai.com/film_school_tai/masters/index.html
Note: This seems to be an M.A. in screenwriting and/or "content" writing.

UNITED KINGDOM

Bath Spa University College
Newton Park, Bath, England
http://ecs.bathspa.ac.uk/prospective/postgrad/MA_creative_writing/overv
iew.html?pagevalue=one
M.A. in creative writing, one year, in poetry, novel, scriptwriting, and writing for young people.

University of Bolton
Bolton, United Kingdom
http://www.bolton.ac.uk/creative/pathways/creativema.html
M.A. in creative writing.
Note: This Web site contained only titles and no information at the time of research.

Cardiff University
Cardiff, Wales, United Kingdom
http://www.cf.ac.uk/encap/creativewriting/index.html
M.A. in the teaching and practice of creative writing. One year in fiction, poetry, creative nonfiction, or scriptwriting.
Note: There were references to a M.Phil in creative writing degree on the Web site, but there were no links and an intensive search found no page to describe such a degree.

University of East Anglia
Norwich, United Kingdom
http://www.uea.ac.uk/eas/admissions/courseprofiles/w800t
M.A. in creative writing in poetry, fiction, screenwriting, or playwriting.

University of Glasgow
Glasgow, Scotland, United Kingdom
http://www.gla.ac.uk:443/studying/pg/prospectus/course.cfm?id=6
MLitt in creative writing.

Lancaster University
Lancaster, United Kingdom
http://www.lancs.ac.uk/depts/cw/ma1intro.htm
M.A. in creative writing, one to two years.
Note: This is not your average graduate program. You'll have to visit the site to see what I mean. Definitely interesting.

University of Manchester
Manchester, United Kingdom
http://www.arts.manchester.ac.uk/subjectareas/englishamericanstudies/pos tgraduatestudy/MAcreativewriting/
M.A. in creative writing in fiction and poetry.

Northumbria University
Newcastle, United Kingdom
http://online.northumbria.ac.uk/prospectus/coursedetail.asp?CourseID=5 12
M.A. in creative writing.
Note: Students have the choice of one year full-time or two years part-time.

Nottingham Trent University
Nottingham, England
http://human.ntu.ac.uk/study_here/postgrad/writing/
M.A. in creative writing, two years, in fiction, poetry, scriptwriting, children's and young adult fiction, creative nonfiction, or new media writing.

Sheffield Hallam
Sheffield, United Kingdom
http://www.shu.ac.uk/schools/cs/english/mawrit.htm
M.A. in writing.

Swansea University
Swansea, Wales, United Kingdom
http://www.swan.ac.uk/english/postgrad/modules
M.A. in creative writing.

Trinity College, University of Wales
Carmarthen, Wales, United Kingdom
http://www.trinity-cm.ac.uk/english/prospectus/pg/macreativewriting.asp
M.A. in creative writing.

University College Winchester
Winchester, United Kingdom
http://www2.winchester.ac.uk/culturalstudies/subjects/english/ma_writ-ing_for_children/

M.A. in writing for children.

Ph.D. Writing Programs Outside the United States

Bath Spa University
Newton Park, Bath, England
http://ecs.bathspa.ac.uk/prospective/postgrad/PHD_creative_writing/over
view.htm?pagevalue=one
Ph.D. in creative writing in fiction, poetry, or playwriting.

University of Calgary
Calgary, Alberta, Canada
http://www.english.ucalgary.ca/creative/
Ph.D. with creative writing option.
Note: "Students should note that because of the high standards expected for
such a project and the department's limited resources in the area of creative
writing, very few students will be able to undertake this creative alternative."

Cardiff University
Cardiff, Wales, United Kingdom
http://www.cardiff.ac.uk/index.html
Note: There is supposedly a Ph.D. in creative and critical writing at Cardiff.
After an exhaustive and frustrating search of the Web site, I finally gave up
the search. I'd expect potential students will do the same until the univer-
sity provides information in a clear and accessible way. An e-mail to the
English department was not returned.

University of Glasgow
Glasgow, Scotland, United Kingdom
http://www.arts.gla.ac.uk/SESLL/EngLit/grad/Creative.html
Ph.D. in English literature and creative writing.

Lancaster University
Lancaster, United Kingdom
http://www.lancs.ac.uk/depts/cw/phd.htm
Ph.D. in creative writing.
Note: This is not your average graduate program. You'll have to visit the site
to see what I mean. Definitely interesting.

University of Manchester
Manchester, United Kingdom
http://www.arts.manchester.ac.uk/subjectareas/englishamericanstudies/pos
tgraduatestudy/phdcreativewriting/
Ph.D. in creative writing in fiction and poetry.

University of New South Wales
Sydney, Australia
http://english.arts.unsw.edu.au/engl/pgresearch_current/cwresdegrees.html
Ph.D. in creative writing.

Swansea University
Swansea, Wales, United Kingdom
http://www.swan.ac.uk/english/research/CWPhD.html
Ph.D. in creative writing.

Warnborough University
Warnborough University is incorporated in the Republic of Ireland as an independent global university for on-site and distance learning.
http://www.warnborough.edu/faculties/arts/mcreative.htm
Ph.D. in creative writing in poetry, fiction, creative nonfiction, or playwriting.
Note 1: Students may study in more than one genre.
Note 2: The program is distance learning, rather than low residency.

Acknowledgments

THE PROBLEM WITH ACKNOWLEDGMENT SECTIONS is that you look forward to writing them, but then you normally wait until the day before the book deadline to get them done. That is the case here. Many people to thank. My sincerest apology for anyone I've left out.

David Roderick was a constant source of advice and encouragement, and he made himself available whenever I had a strange idea or worry about the book. Steve Elliott is always around to lift spirits, offer new perspectives, and in general be a good example of what a writer is and does. Jack and Helen Kealey and their daughter Kerri seemed, to me at least, blindly optimistic when they said, "You'll get it done," though they were, to my great shock and surprise, correct. Thanks to them, and other members of the Kealey and Carroll families who have been so supportive over the years.

Katharine Noel, as I recall, was the first person to say, "That's a great idea," before I actually thought that it was. She was also a great sounding board and source of encouragement, especially in the dangerous early days of the project. In the late dangerous days of the project, that person was Christina McCarroll, who was consistently generous with her time and suggestions. Katie Boyle is a wonderful agent and person, and believed in this book from the get-go. Many thanks to her, and David Barker, and all the people at Continuum Publishing.

Fourteen Stanford students saved me hours and hours and hours of time with their research for the book, at great expense to their own schedules. Their work was thorough, timely, careful, and very insightful. I wouldn't have completed the book without their help. My very sincerest of thanks to Carolyn Abrams, Jennifer Carr, Max Doty, Karen English, Anthony Ha, Jessica Goldman, Jennifer

Kong, Jack Loveridge, Karan Mahajan, Nik Sawe, Andy Orrin, Devmin Palihakkara, Camille Ricketts, and Jenny Zhang.

Over the years many students have offered enthusiasm and insight into this work, before it even was a work. Particular names that come to mind include those above and also Nicholai Lidow, Katie Founds, Vauhini Vara, and Gabriel Kram.

The individuals interviewed for the book were extremely generous with their time, insights, and ideas. Their knowledge and contributions often went far beyond the scope of my questions. I asked many for fifteen minutes and received hours of their time instead. Very special thanks to Aimee Bender, Michael Collier, Victoria Chang, Johanna Foster, Maria Hummel, Adam Johnson, Rachel Kadish, Scott McCabe, Heather McHugh, George Saunders, Tracy K. Smith, Bruce Snider, Peter Turchi, Padma Viswanathan, and Geoffrey Wolff. Rachel, Bruce, and especially Johanna were of great help to me, not only during the interviews, but throughout the course of this project.

I would be remiss if I did not thank my former writing teachers. If there is any knowledge in this book, or in the writing of it, much of it comes from them. Very special thanks to Fred Chappell, John Edgar Wideman, Tobias Wolff, Sam Michel, Noy Holland, Elizabeth Tallent, David MacDonald, Jay Neugeboren, and especially John L'Heureux.

Thanks also to many of my colleagues, whom I've pestered for opinions, insights, research, and support over the years. Early on in my career I counted heavily on Nick Montemarano, Susan Steinberg, and especially Cathy Schlund-Vials. Others who have helped this book in large and small ways are Andrew Altschul, Shara Lessley, Robin Ekiss, Keith Ekiss, Cheryl McGrath, Tom McNeely, Lysley Tenorio, Gaby Calvocoressi, Geoff Brock, Scott Hutchins, Rachel Richardson, Eric Puchner, Sara Martin, Russ Franklin, John Lundberg, Jeff Hoffman, Marika Ismail, Malena Watrous, and Geri Doran. Very special thanks to Adam Johnson.

Thanks also to many supportive people at Stanford not yet mentioned, including Virginia Hess, Mary Popek, Gay Pierce, Matt Jockers, Ruth Kaplan, and Eavan Boland.

General spirit-lifters include Eric and Ashly Morrison, Shaila Djurovich, Kristy Byrd, Matt Alper, Sarah Hinds, Ben Peterson, Wendy McKennon, Christine Texiera, Dawn McAvoy, Chris Kirkman, Allison Jones, Chris Vials, Sandy Chang, Dorothy Hans, Michael Breen, Meena Wilson, Tommy and Kelcie Beaver, and Steadman and Alyssa Harrison.